SECTOR TRADING
STRATEGIES

SECTOR TRADING STRATEGIES

DERON WAGNER

Marketplace Books
Columbia, Maryland

This book, along with other books, is available at discounts that make it realistic to provide them as gifts to your customers, clients, and staff. For more information on these long lasting, cost effective premiums, please call us at 800-272-2855 or e-mail us at sales@traderslibrary.com.

ISBN: 1-59280-307-5
ISBN 13: 978-1-59280-307-1
Printed in the United States of America.

Cover Photo - comstock.com
Art Director/Cover Design - Larry Strauss
Layout Designer - Jennifer Marin

Table of Contents

Sector Trading Strategies

FROM THE PUBLISHER

The editors at Marketplace Books have always kept a steady goal in mind, and that is to present actionable information on stock trading in the most straight-forward, practical medium available. Sometimes this involves a book, sometimes a newsletter, a DVD, or an online course program. What we've learned from the many products we've developed over the years is that a cross-medium approach is the most effective way to offer the greatest possible value to our readers.

So an idea was born. This innovative book and DVD set is one of the first in a series that combines a full course book derived from the actual presentation itself. Our idea grew out of a simple question. Students of stock trading spend a great deal of their own money attending lectures and trade shows. After all the travel, effort, and expense, that student will still have to assimilate a host of often complex theories and strategies. Sometimes he or she may want to ask a question or dig deeper into an issue, but they hold back; maybe because they still don't know enough about the bigger picture or maybe they don't even know some of the basic terminology. They may buy the DVD, but still…a lecture in itself is not a comprehensive learning tool and a person may still need yet another lecture or host of trial and error book purchases to master the subject.

So the question was: Does the average student of trading get enough out of an individual session to effectively carry their studies home and master a subject? The answer was a resounding no! Most attendees get bits and pieces of the message out of a long and expensive lineage of lectures, with critical details hopefully captured in page after page of scribbled notes. For those who are gifted with a photographic memory and vast organizational skills, the visual lecture is just fine, but for the rest of us, the combination of the written word and a visual demonstration is the golden ticket to the mastery of any subject.

A comprehensive approach to learning is the course you are about to embark upon. We've taken Deron Wagner's original lecture and extracted his core content into an easy to read and understand course book. You'll be able to pour over every word of Wagner's groundbreaking presentation, taking in each important point in a step by step, layer by layer process. All of this is possible because our editors have developed this title in classic textbook form.

We've organized and highlighted the key points, added case studies, glossaries, key terms, and even an index so you can go to the information you need when you need it most.

Let's face it, stock trading in any medium takes years to master. It takes time to be able to follow charts and pick out the indicators that mark the wins you'll need to succeed. And beyond the mathematical details and back-tested chart patterns, every presenter has three very basic premises for every student trader; they are to control your emotions, stay close to your trading plan, and do your homework. It's so important to know the full picture of the profession because it could either make you rich or put you in line for that second night job.

This DVD course book package is meant to give you all the visual and written reinforcement you need to study, memorize, document, and master your subject once and for all. We think this is a truly unique approach to realizing the full potential of our Traders' Library DVDs.

As always, we wish you the greatest success.

Meet Deron Wagner

Deron Wagner is the founder and head trader of Morpheus Trading Group. His daily focus is managing and trading the *Morpheus Capital Hedge Fund*, which he founded in April of 2004. He also teaches his trading methodology through several newsletters, including *The Wagner Daily*, *The MTG Stalk Sheet*, and *The Wagner Weekly*.

This book is a companion coursebook for Wagner's best-selling video, *Sector Trading Strategies* (Marketplace Books, June 2002). It discusses one of the often overlooked strategies, that of "sector trading." This is a method in which specific market sectors are targeted and timed to maximize profitability. This book explains how sector trading works; how to follow mutual fund and other institutional trends; how and when to rotate your investment capital; how to identify strong *and* weak sectors; and various methods for entering and exiting from positions (long equity positions, selling short, and using options).

The reputation of some short-term trading strategies (such as day trading and swing trading) has suffered in recent years. This has been due to the activity among some traders leading to unexpected and often very large losses. But remember, when a minority of traders abuses a sound system, it does not mean the system itself is flawed. In this book, you will discover the methodical and sensible path to success in sector trading, including risk analysis and identification of methods for deciding whether a particular strategy is right for you.

Wagner is also co-author of *The Long-Term Day Trader* (Career Press, April 2000) and *The After-Hours Trader* (McGraw Hill, August 2000). Past television appearances include CNBC, ABC, and Yahoo! FinanceVision. He is also a frequent guest speaker at various trading and financial conferences around the world.

The author also is a professional short-term trader and he teaches numerous seminars on sector trading and short-term trading strategies.

For a complimentary trial to Wagner's trading newsletters, or to learn more about the materials contained in this book, please visit www.morpheustrading.com.

Chapter 1

Fundamentals of Sector Trading

The most troubling and most common question people ask me—
"How can I trade this market?" Uncertainty is the most frequently
seen condition, even when some (but not all) of the indicators are
strong. No matter what the overall market did yesterday or last
month, you really have no way to tell which direction the market
will go next.

The problem, though, is that most people judge the market based on
index movement. The Dow Jones Industrial Average, NASDAQ,
and S&P 500 involve the average movement of many stocks. If
half the stocks in the index rise and the other half fall, the net
result is a flat (uncertain) market. Using index measurements is
not accurate for this reason. Just as you cannot rely on the national
averages of housing prices to decide whether the timing is right to
invest in real estate, you need to be able to take a closer look at sectors, parts of the market rather than a collective whole. You need a

more dependable way—not only to time your decisions but also to recognize real trends, in real time, to earn real profits. That's where sector trading becomes a valuable strategy; it provides you with the means for focusing in on a segment of the market, identifying a trend, and then acting.

Some people think they can out-perform the averages by following single stocks, but every stock is affected directly by other stocks in their sectors. Remember, a sector is, by definition, a grouping of companies in the same industry, sharing the same competitive and market challenges, and subject to the same supply and demand cycles.

> **Sector** is the name given to a division of the market, a grouping of companies in the same industry, sharing the same or similar market and competitive factors, and subject to the same supply and demand and business cycles.

The selection of one sector over another, based on business trends and current cyclical strength or weakness, is a sensible way to invest. Using the overall market index is not reliable because these are averages of many stocks. Using single stocks is equally unreliable because each stock follows its sector leaders. In addition, single stocks may or may not act according to the larger sector trend, which is why you also need to know how to pick the best stocks—the leaders—in a sector to ensure that you time decisions properly. In other words, if a sector at large is making a specific move, you need to make sure you pick the right stocks that are leading that trend.

Each sector is defined by characteristics: cyclical business changes, seasonal marketing patterns, and economic trends like interest rates, trade imbalances, and employment. A sector is not just a bunch of companies competing with each other; it is also a grouping of companies subject to the same tendencies, market actions and reactions, and economic and business forces. Sectors can be further broken down into subcategories, and these distinctions are crucial, as I will demonstrate later. The subcategories, may also share distinct and unique models for timing and selection, based on their sub-cycles, sub-economics, and sub-marketing.

My goals in explaining how to trade sectors are to show you how to:

1. Learn how to trade market sectors.
2. Pick specific sectors based on relative strength or weakness.
3. Increase the number of daily trading opportunities.
4. Minimize your risk while maximizing your profits.

All of these goals are realistic and possible, assuming that you are willing to spend the time needed to master the basics and apply sensible rules within a strategic and methodical approach to investing. In this book, I am going to provide you with several important tools in two primary groupings or "lessons." In the first group, I will focus on skills. I'm going to show you how to identify the realm of tradable sectors, pick the most effective technical and fundamental indicators, apply sector rotation strategies, make effective use of sector-tracking indices, and analyze risks to pick the right trading exposure for you. This section concludes with my discussion of four keys to sector trading.

In the last group of lessons, I provide you with three strategic methodologies for achieving effective sector trading profits. First is

More on Sector Rotation:

Sector rotation is an investment strategy that was developed out of the economic data from the National Bureau of Economic Research (NBER). The NBER is the reason that we can quantitatively measure each business cycle. Sam Stovall is one of the leading analysts in the field of sector rotation. As chief investment strategist for Standard & Poor's Corporation, Stovall has an insider's perspective on all of the major sectors and industry groups within the stock market. Using that informational base, he performed a number of historical rotation studies, which led to the publication of his now classic book, *Sector Investing: How To Buy the Right Stock in the Right Industry at the Right Time* (McGraw-Hill, 1996).

According to Stovall (Stone 2005), "The National Bureau of Economic Research sets dates for peaks and troughs in economic activities, based on its assessment of such factors as gross domestic product and employment growth." Stovall posits that the process of dividing the NBER cycles into sub-stages will highlight historically successful periods for stocks in unique sectors; this idea is the foundation of sector rotation analysis.

the best known—the use of equity positions in companies within specific sectors. You can buy stock (go long) or sell stock (go short). The various methods of approaching these two positions contain specific risk elements. You can also use Exchange Traded Funds, or ETFs, to move in and out of specific sectors. ETFs are traded just like stocks but consist of a bundle of stocks usually within the same sector. Finally, you can also use options to leverage your capital within sectors, involving single stocks, indices, or ETFs.

I like to narrow down my guidelines for sector trading into four general areas. These are summarized in Figure 1.1.

Figure 1.1 - Fundamentals of sector trading

- Follow institutional money flow
- Rotate into strong sectors (buy)
- Rotate out of weak sectors (sell short)
- Learn reciprocal relationships

Let's talk about each one of these for a moment.

Follow Institutional Money Flow

The big institutions—mutual funds, pensions, and insurance companies—account for about two thirds of all daily trading volume, as I wrote in "Follow Institutional Traders – Here's How" (see www.tradingmarkets.com). You can learn a lot about the market by how institutions act. The first skill I recommend is that you watch how these companies move billions of dollars in and out of specific sectors. Not only do institutional managers trade sectors continuously; because they are so large, their decisions may impact a sector's strength or weakness.

This is an important point to remember about institutional traders like mutual funds. They buy and sell in huge blocks of stock in single trades; for the individual, or retail investor, this means that the market and the prices of stock are often determined by the timing of institutional managers. If you observe how institutions trade stocks, you will see a cause and effect in sector performance and pricing. This gives you incredible insight about the market and helps you to better time your decisions.

> **For Example:** If all of a sudden Fidelity's accumulating huge positions in the retail stocks—at Wal-Mart, Home Depot, Best Buy, The Gap—then we want to buy those stocks, too. Keep in mind that institutional money flow is going to be what causes a sector to stay strong or a sector to stay weak.

Rotate into Strong Sectors

I encourage you to buy stocks or ETFs in strong sectors. I define a strong sector as one whose potential for price growth is better than average. Later on, I will talk about specific sectors and grouping of sectors that exhibit certain characteristics of strength (or weakness) consistently, based on the same conditions.

Rotate out of Weak Sectors

When people hear my advice to them to rotate out of a sector, they usually think I am suggesting they sell stocks they had previously bought. This is only partially true. You can also initiate a trade by selling short, an alternative way to play the sector market. The attraction of short selling is that it doubles your possibilities for profit. Under traditional buy-hold-sell strategies, you have to buy as the first step, so you are constantly seeking sectors or individual stocks that are oversold and run too high. You then have to wait for prices to fall and accept the possibility that you missed the opportunities. But when you sell short, you reverse the sequence to sell-hold-buy, so you never have to miss an opportunity again. If you start out by identifying a sector that has been run up too high, you can sell short within that sector, wait for prices to fall, and then close the position with a buy order.

Rotating in and out of sectors does not mean selling something you have now and buying something else, although that is certainly one common way to rotate your holdings. It can mean just the opposite. If you are short on a sector, you can rotate by closing your position with a buy order and then either selling or buying a different sector, so rotation is not always replacement. It can also be repositioning—replacing one long position with another or moving from one short to another. Most people tend to rotate by selling A and buying B, or vice versa. But remember, it can go the other way too. Sector trading, especially using multiple strategies and tools, is both flexible and multi-faceted, helping you identify profit potential in both up and down markets.

Learn Reciprocal Relationships

The term reciprocal usually means "I do something for you and you do something for me." However, in the context of sector trading, the definition is slightly different. It means that when one sector is strong, another sector is typically weak and vice versa. I suggest seeking out the signs of offsetting, or reciprocal changes, between dissimilar sectors.

The market, at least in the short-term, tends to favor or disfavor specific sectors in turn. Today the market is hot on tech stocks and cold on pharmaceuticals; next week, the whole thing is turned upside down and the market loves drug companies but wants nothing to do with tech stocks. The tendency is to go back and forth among groups, or sectors. This is not always logical, but it does point you to potential profitable timing. This is a reciprocal arrangement; and among the many strategies sector traders use, recognition of this tendency is important for timing.

Taken together, these four guidelines provide you with a basic appreciation for what I call the fundamentals. But this is only a starting point. You also need to understand how to pick tradable sectors. I will show you how I pick sectors to trade in the next lesson.

Self-test questions

1. Most people judge the current condition of the market based on overall averages and indices such as:

   a. Dow Jones Industrial Averages
   b. The S&P 500
   c. NASDAQ
   d. All of the above

2. A market sector is defined as:

   a. a group of stocks all moving in the same primary trend direction
   b. a group of stocks in the same industry and subject to the same cycles
   c. corporate stocks held up institutional investors (the "public sector")
   d. all stocks in the Dow Jones Industrial Averages

3. Institutional money flow refers to:

   a. the tracking of institutional investments in and out of various sectors
   b. the relative health of a mutual fund's cash flow
   c. profitability among institutional investors on a compound basis
   d. investments made into institutional funds, versus payments made out of the same funds

4. You can rotate out of a weak sector by:

    a. going long on that sector's stock
    b. selling holding you already own or selling short the stocks in the sector
    c. emphasizing only the sector's leaders and selling all other holdings
    d. buying exchange-traded funds for diversification

5. In sector trading, a reciprocal relationship refers to:

    a. agreements among institutional managers to share commissions with major traders
    b. exchanges of profits to facilitate an orderly market
    c. the tendency for some sectors to exhibit strength and, in direct correlation, for other sections to exhibit weakness
    d. any agreement among investors to share and compare information and stock tips

For answers, go to www.traderslibrary.com/TLEcorner

Chapter 2

The Realm of
Tradable Sectors

I know that every investor faces the challenge of picking stocks. You have over 10,000 publicly listed companies to choose from, so where do you begin?

My methodology narrows down the range of selection. Rather than trying to trade 10,000 different stocks, I have narrowed the realm of stocks to about 300 different companies in about 20 different sectors with an additional 68 different subcategories. This is the realm of stocks that we trade on a daily basis.

By narrowing down the list of potential companies, you are able to stay focused on applying not only technical indicators of the different sectors but also fundamental indicators. You are then able to focus on learning fundamental analysis of each of these different stocks in each of these sectors.

> **Technical indicators** are all indicators studying price trends of stock and studying price/volume combinations to anticipate price movement.
>
> **Fundamental indicators** focus on the financial results and status of corporations. Indicators relate to cash flow and valuation, capitalization, and profitability.

To fully appreciate the realm of sectors that Intraday, my company, trades, we have two graphics: one for technology-related stocks and another for non-tech stocks. Let's take a look at the first one in Figure 2.1.

The technology-related stocks are mostly traded on NASDAQ, which, by definition, is a tech-heavy exchange. This fairly large sector has to be broken down into several groups. Since technology is actually not a single sector but an entire market segment, I have identified a series of tech-stock sectors: biotechnology, computer hardware, computer software, computer storage, internet stocks, networkers, semi-conductors, miscellaneous small caps, and wireless.

The top line lists these sectors within the segment. Directly beneath this is the ticker for each sector. For example, Biotech's ticker is $BTK.X. Every sector has a ticker by which you can track that sector's overall market performance. For those sectors that have an associated ticker, this chart provides the symbol. You will note that the Computer Storage sector does not contain a unique symbol of its own.

Next, I have listed the tracking stock in each sector. Some of these sectors are quite broad, so I have narrowed them down for you into sub-sectors. For example, in the Computer Hardware sector,

Figure 2.1: The Realm of Sectors We Trade

TECH STOCKS (MOSTLY NASDAQ)

BIOTECHS — $BTK.X, BBH
- Top-tier Bio Sector Heavyweights: AMGN, BGEN, DNA, HGSI**, IDPH, IMNX, MLNM
- Genetic Mapping Research: AFFX, CRA, GENE, GENZ, IVGN
- Cancer: ABGX, CELG, CEPH, DNA, IMCL, MYGN, VRTX
- Diabetes: INHL
- Heart Disease: CORR
- Neurology: CHIR, ELN
- Infectious: ENZN, GILD, MEDI
- Pharmaceutical Processing: PDLI
- SEPR*

COMPUTER HARDWARE — $IHW.X
- PC Hardware OEM's: AAPL, CPQ, DELL, GTW
- Unix Workstations: HWP, SUNW
- Conglomerates: IBM, LXK
- Manufacturing: FLEX, SANM, JBL, CLS
- Handheld Computing (PDA's): HAND, PALM, RIMM
- Test Hardware: A, TER, TEK

COMPUTER SOFTWARE — $GSO.X, SWH
- Productivity: MSFT, ADBE, INTU, PSFT, SYMC
- eBusiness Apps: BEAS, BVSN, IWOV, SEBL
- EDA - Electronic Design Automation: CDN, SNPS, MENT
- Development Tools: CPWR, RATL
- Application Management: CTXS, MERQ, MUSE, PRGN, QSFT
- Entertainment: ERTS
- Security: CHKP***, RSAS, VRSN****
- Enterprise Database Apps: ORCL, CA
- Manufacturing Support: PMTC

COMPUTER STORAGE
- Fiber-Channel (FC) Equipt: BRCD***, EMLX***, FNSR, JNIC, MCDT
- Storage Hardware: QLGC, EMC, NTAP, SNDK, STK
- Storage Networking Software: LGTO, VRTS
- Storage Peripherals: ADPT

INTERNETS — $IIX.X, HHH
- Mega ISP's: ATHM, AOL, ELNK, AMZN, EBAY**
- Online Advertising: CNET, DCLK, YHOO
- Infrastructure (Web Hosting, Portals, Multimedia): EXDS, RNWK, CMGI***
- B2B: FMKT, INKT, ITWO, PCLN

NETWORKERS — $NWX.X
- Enterprise Networking Equip (Switches/Routers): CSCO, CS, EXTR**, FDRY
- Backbone Routers: AVCI, JNPR***
- Next-Gen Packet Switching & Max'ino Equint: CIEN**, ONIS, SCMR, RBAK
- Optical WAN/Telco Plays (OC-12+): AFCI, ALA, GLW***, JDSU, LU, NT*, SONS
- Cellular Telephone: HWSW, CMVT, ERICY, MOT, NOK, OPWV, QCOM***
- Cable Modem Hardware: SFA

SEMIS — $SOX.X, SMH
- CPU's: AMD, INTC, TMTA
- Graphics-Video: ATVI, ELBO, NVDA*****, PXLW, RMBS, THQI
- Mixed-Signal Datacomm Plays: AMCC***, BRCM***, CNXT, IDTI, PMCS***, RFMD, VTSS, STM, TXCC
- Mixed-Signal: IRF, LLTC, MXIM, IHSM
- Mixed Signal + DSP Conglomerates: ADI, TXN
- Semicustom Logic: ALTR, LSI, MCHP, XLNX
- MEMORY: ATML, CY, MU
- Semi Equipment: AMAT*, ASML, CREE, KLAC, LRCX, NVLS

SMALL CAPS — $RLX.X
- Always check the intraday volume and spread: CVAS, FSII, IDCC, IO, MGL, OIL, SCOR, XOMA, XCAR
- Note: we are just starting to build the small-cap sector so suggestions & input for good smallcap stocks to consider for inclusion is appreciated. Please limit suggestions to average daily volume >100k shares/day.
- Semis - Continued Superconductors: SCON, CDTS, ISCO

WIRELESS — $WSH.X, WMH
- Cellular Voice Service Providers: AWE, NXTL, PCS, VZ
- Wireless Local Area Networks (LANs): AETH, PROX, SBL

intraday investments

Pursuing capital intraday, sleeping well at night.
MASTER STALK LIST (Sector Model)

NOTES:
Hot List
*=Degree of Demonic possession; Devil Stocks

NOTE 7.8.01: The Biotech Sector is tricky to subclassify (segment). This is a preliminary grouping, and we will refine as we research each Company. If you are a Biotech expert, please report for duty on the Biotech sector team!

> **Tracking stock** is the stock that leads a sector or sub-sector; identification is crucial because the tracking stock tends to lead the rest of the sector in price trends.
>
> **Sub-sectors** are broken-down segments of larger, broader sectors into intra-industry specialties for the purpose of defining sectors at a manageable level.

we have identified PC hardware OEM's as one sub-sector, which consists of Apple, Compaq, Dell, and Gateway, which are basically the personal computer manufacturers. Next is the sub-sector UNIX Workstations, which includes two main players: HWP and Sun. This is followed by the Conglomerates sub-sector, including IBM and Lexmark. Additional sub-sectors are Manufacturing with FlexTronics, SA&N, JBL, and CLS; the Handheld Computing sub-sector with Hand, Palm, Rim; and finally, Test Hardware, which includes ATER and TEK. As you can see, my breakdown into sub-sectors is quite detailed and extensive.

I have also listed the trading symbol for Exchange Traded Funds (ETFs) for each sector that has such a fund. Biotechs, computer software, internets, semis, and wireless sub-sectors all have related ETFs, which are identified by their symbols (for example, biotech's ETF is traded under symbol BBH). The ETF is a basket of stocks that trade just like single stocks on the open exchanges and whose portfolio is pre-identified by the stocks in each sector. We will discuss ETFs in more detail in Chapter 8.

The tracking stock for each sector and sub-sector is listed first. The stocks within each sector are directly correlated, and this is the key to understanding why the tracking stock is so important. The trend in a leading company is going to define how the other stocks in the sector behave. Do you think that if Apple and Compaq are strong, Dell and Gateway might also be strong? Absolutely. Look at the biotechs. If CELG, which is in the cancer sub-sector, has some bad news that one of their drugs was not approved by the FDA, do you think it might affect the other six or seven stocks in that sub-sector? Yes, this breakdown lets us track the whole sector based on performance in the tracking stock.

Figure 2.1 is what I call my master stalk sheet. It's not good enough to know just the sectors. It's more important to know the sub-sectors because, on a given day, it might be only three or four sub-sectors that are strong, while the other two or three sub-sectors might not be. Just as you can't track an individual stock by watching the S&P 500, you can't always depend on sector analysis, especially for the larger sectors. You don't want to fall victim to the averaging effect. The way to utilize this graph is to first learn about which stocks reside in a given sub-sector, and then to know how to look at the related stocks. For example, I know that if Dell is strong, I will automatically look at Gateway, Apple, and Compaq. With a little bit of practice—there are only about 300 stocks on here—you can memorize the groupings of stocks and their sub-sectors.

By the way, there are obviously many more stocks that fit into these sub-sectors. The ones listed are the ones that I consider to be tradable. Generally, to meet the test of whether it is tradable, the company has to be liquid enough: it has to trade at least a half of million shares a day, on the average. Most of the stocks listed on the chart trade over a million shares a day.

Figure 2.2: The Realm of Sectors We Trade

OTHER MARKET SECTORS (MOSTLY LISTED)

FINANCIALS			DRUGS & HEALTHCARE		ENERGY COMPLEX				
BANKS & FINANCIALS	BROKERS	CHEMICALS & PRECIOUS METALS	DRUGS	HEALTHCARE	POWER, UTILITIES	OIL COMPANIES	RETAIL	TELCO SERVICE PROVIDERS	
$BKX.X	$XBD.X	$CEX.X	$DRG.X / PPH	$HCX.X	$DUX.X	$XOI.X	$RLX.X	$XTC.X / TTH	

FINANCIALS — BANKS & FINANCIALS ($BKX.X)

Consumer Financial Services: AXP, FNM, FMC
Money Center Banks: BAC, BK, C, FBF, FTU, JPM, ONE
Regional Banks: PNC, PVN, STI, USB, WFC, FITB, KEY, MEL, NCC, NTRS
Insurance Companies ($IUX.X): HUM, UNH, WLP, ALL, AIG, AFL, CNC, SPC, UNM, AET, CB, CI, HIG, LNC, PGC, AOC, PGR, SAFC

BROKERS ($XBD.X)

Traditional Brokers: AGE, GS, LEH, MWD, SCH, MER
Discount Brokers: NITE, AMTD

CHEMICALS & PRECIOUS METALS ($CEX.X)

Chemical Manufacturing: APD, PX
Plastic & Rubber: MMM, DD, ROH, DOW
Precious Metals: ABX, ECO, HM, PDG, NEM

DRUGS ($DRG.X / PPH)

Major Drug Companies: BMY, JNJ, LLY, MRK, PFE
Second Tier: ABT, AHP, PHA, TTP, SGP

HEALTHCARE ($HCX.X)

Healthcare Equipment and Supplies: BAX, BSX, GDT, MDT, STJ
Healthcare Facilities: HCA, THC

POWER, UTILITIES ($DUX.X)

Power Sector (High Beta): ETR, CPN
Alternative Energy: FCEL, PLUG, BLDP, HPOW, BCON, IMCO
Traditional Utilities: EPG, WMB, SO, DUK, AEP, DUK

Note: We are just starting to build out the ENERGY sector, a lot of changes pending in the next release of this spreadsheet. Input welcome from knowledgeable Intraday members.

OIL COMPANIES ($XOI.X)

Oil Producers: AHC, CHV, KMG, MRO, OXY, P, RD, SUN, TX, UCL, XOM
Oil Service (Drillers) ($OSX.X): BHI, CAM, DO, HAL, KMG, NE, PTEN, RIG, SII, SLB, TDW

RETAIL ($RLX.X)

Department / Discount Stores: MAY, FD, WMT, TGT, S, JCP, KSS
Grocery Stores: ABS, KR, SWY
Drug Stores: RAD, CVS, WAG
Electronics Stores: RSH, BBY, CC
Apparel Stores: ROST, GPS, LTD, ANF, TLB
Specialty Stores: BBBY, SPLS, COST, TOY
Home Improvement: LOW, HD
Consumer (non-cyclical): KKD, MCD, KO, SBUX

TELCO SERVICE PROVIDERS ($XTC.X / TTH)

ILEC's (Incumbent): AT, BLS, SBC, Q, VZ
Major IXC's (Inter-Exchange Carriers): DT, FON, T, TMX, WCOM
CLEC's (Competitive Local Exchange Carriers): BRW, GX, LVLT
Wireless Svc Providers: AWE, VOD, PCS

NOTES:
Hot List

intraday investments

investing capital between sleeping well at night.

MASTER STALK LIST (Sector Model)

Secondly, I like the stocks I consider tradable to be somewhat volatile. For example, Disney is not on any of my stalk sheets because it moves about 20 cents a day. You can't really trade it because it lacks the requisite volatility for my system. The companies listed are the stocks that meet my strict criteria. On a daily basis, if a stock is not on my stalk sheet, I don't trade it. I limit my trading to only what is listed. This keeps me very focused and prevents me from getting distracted. Like everyone else, I hear all about all the stocks people are talking about, but I have my hard-and-fast rule—if it's not on my sub-sector list, I don't trade it.

A second group, the non-tech stocks, is summarized on Figure 2.2

These represent the majority of non-tech stocks that we watch in nine sectors: banks and financials, brokers, chemicals and precious metals, drugs, healthcare, power and utilities, oil companies, retail, and telco service providers. Just like our complex of tech stocks, these nine sectors are further broken down into sub-sectors.

While our sector classifications are ever-changing and evolving, our latest breakdown among sectors and sub-sectors for all the sectors that we watch is summarized in Appendix A.

Appendix A, Table 1 gives you a good idea of how I see the market and, more specifically, the market for sector trading. I have previously mentioned that I view these stocks using both technical and fundamental indicators; this is crucial because together these define how a sector gets on the list and which stocks end up as tracking stocks within sectors and sub-sectors.

It is the combination of these two classes of indicators that I use for identification of stocks within sectors, the timing of moves, and the status of the overall sector. The next section briefly explains the technical and fundamental indicators most valuable for sector trading; after that, I want to take the discussion forward to some sector rotation strategies.

Self-test questions

1. Technical indicators are:

    a. too complex for the average investors, requiring computer price modeling

    b. those emphasizing price trends and charting of price and volume

    c. based on thorough analysis of financial statements of companies

    d. used only for business budgeting and never for investing

2. Fundamental indicators are:

    a. all indicators used by individual investors but not by institutions

    b. those emphasizing price trends and charting of price and volume

    c. based on thorough analysis of financial statements of companies

    d. any indicators expressed in plain English

3. A tracking stock is:

    a. the stock tracked in sector trading because it is the leader of its sector

    b. any stock used in technical analysis to anticipate changes in price direction

    c. used primarily in calculating 200-day moving averages for trend tracking

    d. the highest-beta stock in any sector, which tends to set the volatility level for all stocks in the sector

4. A sub-sector is:

    a. a further breakdown of a sector into a smaller series of groups

    b. a sector whose stocks are inferior and not useful; for sector trading

    c. any distinct group of stocks with lower than average volatility levels

    d. a sector consisting of spun-off subsidiaries of conglomerates

5. A master stalk sheet is:

    a. used solely in commodities trading, and the name is derived from the 19th century when prices of corn stalks were tallied by hand

    b. the computerized listing of all market sectors, arranged in order of beta, with highest beta sectors shown first

    c. the network of insiders and corporate executives experienced sector traders use to discover hidden opportunities

    d. the sheet listing sectors, sub-sectors and tracking stocks used in sector trading

For answers, go to www.traderslibrary.com/TLEcorner

Chapter 3

Technical and Fundamental

I like to use a combination of indicators to pick sectors and stocks within those sectors. In this lesson, I will briefly summarize what I consider the key indicators in both types of analysis; but remember, this is just an overview. If you want a more detailed explanation, you should refer to one of the many books on these topics.

Technical Indicators

Technical indicators involve only the study of a stock's price and volume. To get some good short-term price action, I have discovered that stocks have to contain at least a moderate level of volatility, meaning the trading range of the stock is substantial enough to see some price movement every day. By volatility, I mean the breadth of the trading range. If a stock trades every day within one or two points, it isn't very useful for short-term trading; there simply isn't enough movement.

> **Volatility** is a measurement of price movement. The more point spread in the movement, the greater the volatility. For sector trading, a degree of volatility is needed to create movement.
>
> **Trading range** is the area between established high and low trading prices of a stock. The range indicates the degree of volatility, or "breadth," of trading and provides a distinction between low- and high-volatility stocks.

Volatility is normally associated with the market risk of a particular stock. The greater the volatility, the greater the risk. This is true; but, opportunity is the flip side of risk. You need that volatility to get short-term price movement and to earn and then take profits. Volatility is a matter of judgment; you might find yourself attracted to highly volatile stocks or only to stocks with a moderate degree of volatility.

The distinction of volatility between one stock and another can be made in several ways. One popular, but inaccurate, method is to base volatility on a 12-month summary of a stock's overall trading range. The difference between high and low prices is divided by the low to find the percentage of volatility. For example, if a stock traded during a 12-month period between 42 and 57, its volatility calculated under this method is 36%:

$$(57 - 42) \div 42 = 36\%$$

There are several flaws in this method. First, much can happen in those 12 months. An accurate measurement of volatility should include a check of a stock's price chart for the past 12 months. If the price spiked at any time, then I would prefer to measure volatility without the spike. Let's say that this stock with a price range from 57 down to 42 actually traded for the entire year between 42 and 48 but spiked up to 57 on a single day. As long as the price returned to its previously established trading range, I would want to remove the spike and recalculate:

$$(48 - 42) \div 42 = 14\%$$

This percentage is quite different from the 36% calculated under the popular method. I also don't like the 12-month method because it gives you the range but doesn't tell you what that range actually means. Consider the following possible scenarios:

1. The stock moved from a low 12 months ago to its high most recently.
2. The stock moved from a high 12 months ago to its low most recently.
3. The stock traded very flat most of the year with short-term expansion above and below an otherwise narrow trading range.

Of course, any number of scenarios is possible, and they all mean different things; hence, using a 12-month range (more frequently called a 52-week high/low) is unreliable and inaccurate.

This makes a big difference in the conclusions you draw about a stock. This is true because the trading range for any stock is the most critical feature to technical analysis. Action of the price within this range provides you with signals of price movement above or below the range, called a breakout. When the top or bottom is

> **Resistance level** is the top price of the trading range, or the highest price that buyers are willing to pay to acquire shares.
>
> **Support level** is the lowest price or the bottom of the trading range; the lowest price that sellers are willing to accept to give up shares.

tested two or more times without a breakout, it usually indicates that the price is about to begin moving in the opposite direction.

A breakout can take several different forms. If there is a trading gap between the previously established trading range and the breakout range, the trend is strong. If you study technical analysis in depth, you will discover that many variations of gaps and related signals are considered to be very important by technicians.

The range in which a stock trades is defined by its top and bottom prices. At the top is the resistance level, which is the maximum price level buyers are willing to spend to acquire shares. At the bottom is the support level, which is the lower price at which sellers are willing to give up shares. As long as these levels hold, the trading range remains intact. Technicians are continually checking for signs that the price is going to move away from the established trading range.

Resistance and support are the crux of virtually all technical analysis and the theories surrounding it. The range defines the stock not only in terms of its risk and volatility but also by the significance of price movement itself. Identifying levels of resistance and support, those technical "lines in the sand," means that any price movement that breaks through those levels is, indeed, very important. Interpreting these movements that violate resistance and support are the lifeblood of technical analysis.

The chartist is a technician who looks for price patterns to time the purchase or sale of stock. In many respects, the chartist is the priest of the technical faith.

Of the various types of chart patterns that we trade, the Head and Shoulders is one of the most reliable and profitable types of setups. Let's begin by looking at a basic diagram of a Head and Shoulders pattern (Figure 3.1).

The head and shoulders pattern occurs when the price reaches a specific price twice (the shoulders), interspaced with a higher price level (the head). Once the head and shoulders pattern occurs, chartists interpret the pattern to mean that prices are going to move in the opposite direction.

A head and shoulders pattern (hereafter H&S) is a bearish reversal chart pattern that often marks the top of an uptrend and predicts a selloff in a particular index or ETF. The left shoulder and head are formed as the index is rallying and does not indicate anything bearish. However, once the neckline is formed on the right side of the head, that is our first warning sign that the buying momentum has slowed because rather than setting a higher low on the previous rally, the index sells off all the way down to the prior low. When this occurs, people who bought near the top (the head) are now trapped in the long position. Then, as another wave of buyers attempt to rally the index, the people who are trapped long at the top sell into the rally in an attempt to just come close to breaking even. This weakens the index even more, which prevents the achievement of a higher high and also forms the right shoulder. This usually marks a break of the uptrend as the index comes back

FIGURE 3.1

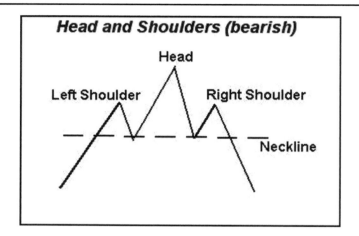

down once again and tests the prior low. At this point, everyone who bought on the left shoulder, head, and right shoulder are now trapped and out of the money in their positions. So guess what happens? They begin to sell, which causes a break of the neckline, which subsequently causes a rapid and often volatile collapse of the price due to selling momentum.

Although the most ideal entry point for shorting a H&S pattern can be debated, I prefer to enter after the right shoulder has been formed and starts back down to the neckline. If you enter before the right shoulder is formed, there is not enough confirmation that there really is a H&S pattern being formed, so you will often stop yourself out by shorting too soon. On the other hand, if you wait for the neckline to break before selling short, your entry price is not that great and can often result in getting shaken out of the position right before it cracks or in missing the selloff altogether. However, by shorting after the right shoulder has been formed and the price starts coming back down, you are essentially selling into strength, which gives you a lower risk and higher profit entry point. If the H&S fails and does not follow through, your losses are also reduced because you shorted at a decent price. Remember that the goal of our trading strategy is not to squeeze every single dollar of profit out of a trade, but rather to catch a bulk of the profits with minimal risk.

When a H&S drops below the neckline (which is sometimes ascending or descending), the predicted selloff amount is usually equal to the distance from the top of the head down to the neckline. So, if the price at the top of the head is $100 and the price at the neckline is $90, the predicted drop would be equal to $10 (100 - 90) below the neckline. Since the neckline is $90, the predicted selloff is down to $80. This is a guideline you can use to determine a target price for where to take profits on a short setup.

Although H&S patterns follow-through a majority of the time, there are occasions when the pattern fails, meaning that it never drops below the neckline after forming the right shoulder (Figure 3.2). A failed H&S pattern occurs when the price rallies above the high of the head after forming the right shoulder. When the price rallies above the head, make sure you quickly cut your losses if you are short because the move is usually strong if there were enough buyers to propel through all that resistance and set a new high. After getting through the resistance of the H&S pattern, the failed short setup often becomes a great long play. Figure 3.2 is an example of a failed H&S.

One indicator you can use to assist in determining the probability of whether or not the H&S will follow-through is volume. As with every other type of chart pattern, volume is the most critical type of technical analysis, and this pattern is no different. Specifically, what we look for is lighter volume on the right shoulder than on the left shoulder. If volume on the formation of the right shoulder is significantly less than the volume that formed the left shoulder, it indicates there are less buyers to rally the index, which increases the probability of coming back down to test the neckline and eventually breaking below it. Conversely, increasing volume on the right shoulder is often a warning sign that the pattern may not follow-through and we will need to cover our shorts if the right shoulder ends up breaking above the head.

FIGURE 3.2

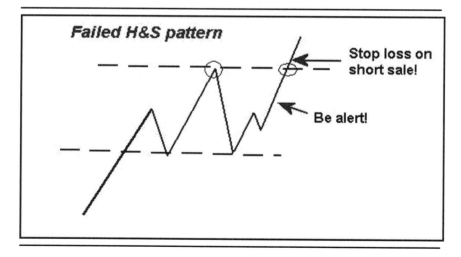

It is important to realize that the amount of time it takes an index or ETF to complete the breakdown of the H&S pattern is largely dependent on the time frame of which the setup occurs. For example, a H&S pattern that sets up on a 5-minute intraday chart will usually follow through and complete the selloff within a few hours. However, if you see a H&S on a sixty-minute chart, it will probably take several days or even a week to complete the predicted drop. A H&S on a daily chart will usually take weeks or even months to follow-through. Therefore, if you see a H&S pattern on a daily chart, it's typically not as easy as blindly going short unless you are the type of trader who can stomach volatility. If you short a H&S on a daily chart, you will probably stop yourself out unless you allow the setup a significant amount of time and price volatility before it follows-through. Because of this, we prefer to trade H&S patterns that occur on shorter time frames such as 15 or 60 minute charts. These make for ideal swing trades on the short side and are often the source of short setups for ETFs listed in my Wagner Daily newsletter.

There is a bullish variation of the H&S pattern that is called an Inverse Head and Shoulders pattern (Figure 3.3). This pattern is identical to the H&S pattern detailed above except that it is flipped upside down. The predicted move to the upside is also the distance from the head to the neckline, just like with a regular H&S.

There are many additional technical indicators useful for sector trading. This is simply a look at the basics.

FIGURE 3.3

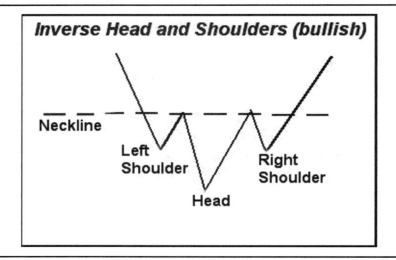

Fundamentals Indicators

Fundamentals indicators are all indicators compiled from financial information. These indicators are formed into ratios or expressions of financial results. Just like the technical side, there are dozens of valuable fundamental indicators. Among those that I consider the most important are a few that I divide into three groups: working capital, capitalization, and profitability.

A working capital ratio demonstrates how effectively a company makes use of its cash flow to fund operations and growth. The most popular working capital ratio is called the current ratio. This is a comparison between current assets (cash and assets convertible to cash within one year) and current liabilities (the company's debts payable within 12 months). A working capital of 2 to 1 or better is considered standard; anything below that level implies possible working capital problems. In other words, you expect the company to report two dollars of current assets for every dollar; it's current liabilities at the end of each reporting period.

A capitalization ratio examines the sources of a company's funding. There are two kinds of capitalization: debt and equity. Debt capitalization is the long-term borrowings of a company, usually called bonds on the balance sheet. Equity capitalization is the value of capital stock plus retained earnings (accumulated profits) over the company's history. The most important capitalization ratio is the debt ratio, which is a percentage of long-term debt over the sum of long-term debt and stockholders' equity. As the portion of total capitalization rises, there is less profit left over to pay dividends; thus, a well-managed company should maintain its debt ratio steadily over the years.

The final group, the profitability ratio, is any test of revenues and profits. The most popular among these is the net return, a percentage of net profits to revenues. Additional profitability ratios involve tracking growth in revenues, gross profits, and expenses as a means for determining how effectively management controls market expansion and exercises internal controls.

It is also revealing to study the operating statement and to look for specific trends. For example, you would expect to see rising sales and profits in a well-managed company; but all too often, you see that even when sales rise, expenses rise more quickly, resulting in higher sales but lower profits. This is a danger signal, indicating that management is unable to exercise internal controls. Higher sales lead to higher spending unless those controls are held in check; so among the most important monitoring routines in fundamental analysis is watching the relationship between sales and costs and between sales and expenses.

This brief overview of technical and fundamental indicators provides a glance at the kinds of tests I apply to stocks within sectors and sub-sectors. In the next sector, I will explain how changes in these indicators lead to the strategic application of sector rotation.

Self-test questions

1. A stock's trading range is:

   a. the difference between book value per share and the current market price per share of stock

   b. the sector or range of competing companies within the same sector

   c. the difference between a stock's lowest and highest price, also known as support and resistance

   d. the high and low prices the stock has traded over the past 12 months

2. Resistance and support are references to:

   a. acceptability of a stock or sector to institutional investors

   b. a stock's low and high points within its trading range

   c. alternate terms for PE ratio and earnings per share

   d. the range of the PE ratio over the past 12 months

3. The term "head and shoulders" refers to:

    a. collectively, the CEO and senior executive staff of
        a company
    b. a trading pattern caused by excessive institutional trading
        within a sector.
    c. a dangerous sign that a stock's price is about to
        fall drastically
    d. a trading pattern consisting of two plateaus (shoulders)
        interspaced by a higher or lower price level (the head)

4. The current ratio is:

    a. a factor comparing current assets to current liabilities.
    b. simply the latest ratio in a series
    c. a ratio showing the differential between current and long-
        term debt
    d. a profitability test in which current year net earnings are
        reported as a percentage of the previous year's net earnings

5. The debt ratio demonstrates:

    a. the level of total debt as a percentage of net earnings
    b. the dollar amount of short-term debt to current assets
    c. the percentage of long-term debt to the combined totals
        of long-term debt and stockholders' equity
    d. the percentage of annual interest payments made on out-
        standing bonds

For answers, go to www.traderslibrary.com/TLEcorner

Chapter 4
Sector Rotation Strategies

You can employ both technical and fundamental indicators to identify when specific sectors or stocks are (a) strong, (b) weak, or (c) neutral. Remember, the key to sector trading is that some sectors will out-perform the market and others will lag behind. In fact, this is always the case on any trading day and in any market condition. Sector rotation is an important element to my strategy because the status of every sector is continually changing.

In fact, rotation is a requirement in order to put my three-part sector trading strategy to work. In this strategy, I am able to (1) identify which market sectors are the strongest, (2) determine which stocks lead that trend within top-performing sectors, and (3) sell short those sectors lagging behind. Because of the constant state of flux in the market, I need to review this strategy continuously.

This triple-play approach works in all markets and investment climates. You need to be able to rotate in and out of sectors as conditions change. The key to understanding sector rotation is to act based on the fact that, typically, investment money flows out of one sector and into another. For example, money flowing out of the technology stocks (a very broad category consisting of semi-conductors, networks, and hardware) will move into drug stocks in major pharmaceuticals. The reason for this is that drug stocks are *old economy* whereas tech stocks are *new economy*; so there is a tendency for capital to move from one to the other. Old economy stocks are generally considered to be a little more of a safe haven when the market is volatile. The demand for pharmaceutical companies is always going to be there. When investors are nervous or shaken up about tech stocks, you'll often see an offsetting increase in value in the drug sector. This relationship is only one of many examples.

Old economy is a set of companies that have been around for a long time and offer products that will always be in demand.

New economy refers, in a broad sense, to the tech stocks; these companies provide products and services that did not even exist 50 years ago and that are not always necessities, so demand tends to change cyclically for these stocks.

Another example can be made of oil and oil service company stocks, in the transportation sector. There is a very specific reason for the relationship between these two—if the price of oil goes up and oil rallies, guess what happens to transports? They go down. These reciprocal relationships are invariably based on common sense. If you can discover these reciprocal relationships, this knowledge will greatly enhance your trading profitability.

A third rotation play I like to watch is change within t
market, in gold and utilities. These two are considered s
in rough times. During times when the markets are g ...g ...t
(when the indices are moving downward strong) gold stocks are
often on a tear. Utility stocks do the same. There is a tendency,
when people are nervous about stocks in general, to want to move
to stocks perceived to be safer.

When the technology bull market ended in 1999, money was flowing out of the tech stocks and into utilities. At that time, I traded
utilities stocks for three months straight, and many of those stocks
rose 100% in that time period. Ironically, because emphasis on the
tech sector was so strong, many people didn't even realize there was
such a strong rally in utility stocks. Learning to spot these reciprocal relationships will help you a lot with your trading and with
improving your broader view of the market.

I have summarized the three sector rotation markets, explained
in Figure 4.1.

Logic works in both directions, so the inverse of these relationships
is true. If money is going out of the drugs, it will often move into

---

Figure 4.1 - Typical Sector Rotation

Out Of	Into
Technology Sectors	Drugs
Oil	Transports
Broader MArket	Gold/Utilities

Obviously, the inverse of these relationships is also true.

---

technology. It's common sense. The cyclical mood of the markets makes sector rotation a sensible—and profitable—strategy.

You don't have to buy the whole sector. Later, I will show you how you can do that using Exchange Traded Funds. An effective strategy involving sector rotation focuses only on a sector's tracking stock. Remember, the tracking stock tends to lead the rest of the sector, so if your sector rotation call is accurate, you can do well by trading only that one issue. For example, let's say you have identified a particular sector you want to move into on the long (buy) side. You can buy the tracking stock of that sector, rather than trying to buy into the entire thing.

Figure 4.2 - Sector Tracking Stocks (holders):

QQQ (Nasdaq 100)

SPY (Spyder/S&P 500)

DIA (Diamonds/DJIA)

BBH (Biotech)

PPH (Drugs)

SMH (Semis)

SWH (Software)

TTH (Telecom)

WMH (Wireless)

HHH (Internets)

OIH (Oil Service)

ron Wagner

This works on the short side as well. If you identify a sector you believe is going to be weak, you can sell the tracking stock rather than try to short numerous stocks within the sector. Incidentally, not every sector has a tracking stock. Figure 4.2 summarizes the tracking stocks that you can use for sector rotation.

To summarize how the entire strategy works, remember that sector trading depends on your ability to use rotation and to recognize how money tends to move between offsetting sectors.

I'd like to end this section by summarizing the four keys to successful sector trading.

4 Keys to Sector Trading

- Always trade with the trend of the markets
- Trade sectors showing the most relative strength or weakness to the markets
- Trade the leaders, not the laggards
- Remember that volume speaks volumes!

Always Trade with the Trend of the Markets

These trends involve the cause and effect of rotation between sectors. Money tends to move in predictable ways, and this movement is what sets trends. Once you observe this fact, you are better able to profit from rotation and to make sector trading a powerful investment strategy.

Essentially, the plan is simple—you can buy sectors that are strong and sell short sectors that are weak. Do you think it makes more sense to sell short a sector as the market is rallying or do you think it makes sense to find a strong sector and buy it as the market is rallying? Which do you think is a better risk reward? The answer is obvious; however, look around at how people invest, and you'll see that a lot of investor programming leads to making the wrong decisions based on market timing. Buying a sector when the market is rallying is going to give you better *risk-reward ratio* than trying to find a weak sector and sorting that sector as the market is rallying.

> **Risk-reward ratio** is the inescapable connection between potential loss and potential profit. The higher the risk, the greater the opportunity, and vice versa.

The opposite applies if the market is selling off. You are going to be more likely to have a profitable experience if you sell short a relatively weak sector than if you buy a sector that's going up.

One way to minimize risk is by going with the overall trend of the market. That is, if intra-day the market is going down, you're going to look to sell short the weak sectors. If intra-day the markets are going up, you look to buy the strong sectors. It's pretty simple.

Trade Sectors Based On Relative Strength or Weakness

There is a specific reason to focus on the strongest trends. They are more easily spotted and your potential profits will be greater.

What you need to do to identify relative strength or weakness is to set up a chart that shows two different things at the same time. One trend follows the sector and the other tracks the broader market (based, for example, on S&P futures). If the market falls off a cliff and your sector just rallied to a new high, obviously that's a relatively strong sector. By setting up and configuring your charts in this manner, it makes it very simple at a glance to know whether those sectors are relatively strong or relatively weak.

Don't make the mistake of confusing the percentage a sector is up or down on the day with whether that sector is strong or weak. For example, let's look at the semi-conductors sector. Let's say Intel comes out with good news prior to the open. The semiconductor index may gap up 5%. Within the first ten minutes of trading, the semi-conductor index is up 5% on the day. Now, we fast-forward to 3:30 p.m. Eastern time, half an hour before the market closes. Let's say the semi-conductor sector is still up 5% on the day. Meanwhile, the NASDAQ has rallied from opening at plus-20 to plus-120, but the semi-conductor index is still only up 5%. Well, does that mean that sector that day had relative strength or not? No, it was up 5% on the day, but that sector didn't necessarily have relative strength because it wasn't moving with the market. It gapped up and stayed there.

Be careful not to look at just how much a sector is up or how much a sector is down. It's more important to know how that sector is trading in relation to the overall futures markets. I don't really care what percentage a sector is up or down. The important thing is that the sector has strength. That's really what should be emphasized.

Trade the Leaders, Not the Laggards

My master stalk sheet (Figures 2.1, 2.2) makes this a little bit easier for you. The sub-sector category groupings help identify the actual sector leaders and break down the sector into more manageable groupings. If you are trading the drug stocks, for example, the leader is generally going to be a stock like Merck versus a stock like American Home Products (AHP). Why is that? Why are the leaders better to trade than the laggards?

When institutional money rotates into a particular sector, it is generally going to go to the leaders of that sector. If the semi's are strong, typically you are not going to have a very strong rally in the sector unless Intel is up, for example. In the drug sector, Merck will tend to be a leader in the same way and for the same reasons.

One mistake that I made when I first was learning this methodology—and it's a very easy mistake to make—was to follow the daily point change in a stock. I'd say to myself, "It's 2:00 in the afternoon. Sysco is already up four points on the day; it's already up 6%. Man, I don't want to get in that stock. It had already moved so much; let me see if I can find something that hasn't moved yet."

So, I would look for another stock in the same sub-sector. I would find Foundry Networks, AFDRY. That stock might be up only half a percent on the day. I would buy that stock, telling myself, "This one hasn't caught up to the rest." For the remaining two hours, I would watch Sysco go up another point and a half while my stock went up only a penny. There is a reason that the leader of the sector is strong. That's where money is going. Don't make the mistake of buying a stock that hasn't moved yet because you think it's going to catch up with the leader. Generally, there's a reason it's not rallying.

I don't care if a stock is already up one point or five points on a day. If there is volume and strength, it's going to keep going higher. There's no worse feeling than getting into the one stock in a sector that doesn't move when everything else in that sector is moving. That's what happens if you don't trade the leaders of the sector.

The same principle applies on the short side. Generally, your less prominent players in the market are going to be the ones that sell off first; and, therefore, they will be the better ones to short than the market leaders. It stands to reason that the last ones to fall are usually the market leaders like the blue chips or the large caps.

Remember that Volume Speaks Volumes

Volume is a crucial indicator. It should be number one on your list. In fact, before we had high-tech charting capabilities, that's how people traded. Traders would look at price and volume action, and they could very easily, very profitably, make money trading stocks based upon price and volume interaction. I've actually used that technique where, due to technical problems, I didn't have any charts and all that was available was a level-one ticker. All I could see was the volume and the price on a stock, but I was able to profitably trade by looking at those two indicators together.

By volume, I don't mean just the number of shares the stock normally trades in a day. I am looking at this in terms of what the volume is today versus its average. For example, let's say you are looking at a stock that normally trades one million shares a day. Within the first half hour of the market being open, the stock's already traded a half million shares. Do you think that stock is going to end up having higher than average volume that day? Obviously, if it's traded half of its average daily volume in the first half hour, then that stock is probably going to do 300 or 400% of its average volume.

On the other hand, let's say you are looking at stock that normally trades five million shares a day. At 2:00 p.m. Eastern time, you've got two hours left in the session and that stock has only traded 1.8 million shares; therefore, it's probably going to come in on a less than average volume day.

The stocks that I want to be in are those stocks that are showing higher-than-average volume; not lower-than-average volume. Here is the rule of thumb that I use. It's general and can probably be modified to your personal preference. I like to make sure that the stock I enter is on target to do at least 125% of the average daily volume of the past five days. So, if over the past five days the stock has averaged four million shares a day, I would only want to get in that stock if it looked as if it were on track to do at least five million shares of volume, or 125% above its average.

Why is volume so important? Why is it so crucial? You can think of volume as being the momentum needed to keep a stock strong or, if you're short, to keep a stock weak. Another mistake I made when I first started learning the system was that I would look at relative strength and say, "Wow, this stock looks great. The market is going sideways, and my stock just keeps rallying to new highs. Let me buy this stock." I would forget to look at what? Volume. That's a big mistake to make because that stock might not be strong because there are a lot of buyers; or it may simply be there is a lack of sellers, so that the stock is not as strong as it appears. You want to condition yourself to determine first whether the stock has relative strength or weakness and then to check its volume.

You know if the stock is trading less than its average volume, it may look like it's strong. It's trending up nicely throughout the whole day. But let's suppose a big fund like Fidelity decided to unload a large size position of that stock. If the volume is light and you get one big sell order, that stock that's relatively strong can take a rather big dive in a matter of minutes because there are not enough buyers out there to sustain the selling level. The same works on the opposite side when the volume is healthy. If the stock is trading on 200% of its average daily volume and Fidelity decides to sell a big block of that stock, there are going to be more buyers to absorb the selling pressure that hits, so the stock is less likely to sell off; in fact, it might not be affected at all. It might drop an eighth or a quarter instead of a point.

Another question concerning volume: How do you know if the stock is on pace to do more than its average volume? If you use multiple timeframes of charting, that's how you know. For example, if you are 15 minutes into the day's open, look at a five-day chart, a three-minute intra-day chart that goes back five days, and the first five bars of the past five days. You can just eyeball the trend quickly. You can tell immediately if the stock is generating more than its average volume. You can just use different intra-day timeframes to see that.

Volume is just as important on the short side. We said we don't want to buy a stock unless it's trading 125% or more of its average daily volume of the past five days. You may be looking at a stock that's just been going down all day; but again, it might not be that there are a lot of sellers. It just might be there are not many buyers out there. Your question should be, "Is the sell volume heavy or is it just that there are not many buyers out there?" I would rather be short on a stock that's selling off in high volume than sell short a stock that's selling off in light volume.

In the next section, I will expand these explanations by showing you some actual sector tracking indices that I use.

Self-test questions

1. The three-part sector trading strategy involves:

   a. thorough stock selection, narrow-range PE ratio, and emphasis on blue chips

   b. buying into strong sectors, focusing on stocks leading the trend, and selling lagging market sectors

   c. timing the market by working only in exceptionally strong sectors, avoiding weak sectors, and using exchange traded funds for diversification

   d. working from the master stalk sheet, using rotation to offset market trends, and acting as a contrarian against the broader market

2. The key observation for sector rotation is:

   a. investment money tends to flow predictably from specific sectors into other specific sectors

   b. smart investors reinvest profits to achieve compound returns and rotate profits into ever-higher increments

   c. no single sector remains a leader forever, but tends to go in and out of favor cyclically; therefore, investors need to rotate capital periodically

   d. capital should be rotated in and out of issues based on trading hour because a day's trend in each sector is established in the first 45 minutes of the trading day

3. The terms "old economy" and "new economy" refer to:

   a. sources of capitalization between family money and newer leveraged entrepreneurial funding

   b. outdated modes of analysis, including traditional fundamentals and EBIDTA versus computer-modeled stock analysis and charting

   c. older companies whose products are obsolete versus more dynamic new approaches to market competitiveness

   d. sectors that have been around for a long time which tend to sell necessities versus the newer tech sectors that tend to perform more cyclically

4. Trading with the market trend simply means:

   a. following market tendencies and investing in the same way

   b. investing primarily in mutual funds with strong historical results

   c. buying strong sectors and selling weak sectors

   d. all of the above

5. The best way to interpret volume trends is:

   a. analyze current volume in comparison to the stock's recent average volume

   b. to focus on only those stocks with consistent day-to-day volume trends

   c. only watch sector-wide volume without the distraction of volume in individual stocks

   d. to consider changes in volume as valid only after the new levels are established for at least three trading days

For answers, go to www.traderslibrary.com/ TLEcorner

Chapter 5
Sector Tracking Indices

Most of us learn better visually than by other means. With this in mind, I have put together a few charts showing how I use and interpret information. These tracking indices are what I use each day. Most of them are *candlestick charts*, which show at a glance the day's high and low trading range, direction of movement, opening and closing price, and volume.

> **Candlestick charts** are valuable technical tools showing a stock's daily high and low prices, trading range, direction of movement, opening and closing prices, and volume.

Most examples of short-term trading—day or swing trading and, of course, sector trading—are aided with candlestick charts. It is valuable to combine candlesticks with 50-day and 200-day moving averages so that an analyst or investor can see at a glance how short-term and daily trades converge with longer-term trends.

The first chart I am going to show you has neither candlesticks nor moving averages. I have avoided these because, in this example, I want to show you the price movements of two different stocks and, in such instances, candlesticks can be a little confusing.

I find it far easier to use a line chart for any side-by-side comparisons, and this is also a valuable way to study sector trading. I actually study seven or eight different charts before deciding to enter

FIGURE 5.1 - Oil Sector vs. S&P 500 Futures

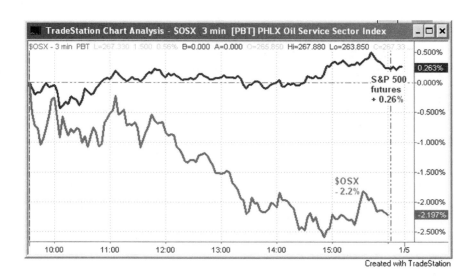

Source - TradeStation

a trade, so I depend heavily on charting as a tool for making my trading decisions.

In Figure 5.1, you see a chart I use to compare relative strength or weakness to the movement of the S&P 500 Futures. In this example, the oil service sector price movement (the more volatile line) is compared to the S&P 500 Futures, rising through the charted period. I find that the S&P is a somewhat better comparative indicator than the Dow or NASDAQ.

Overlaying a sector to the S&P allows you to look for *divergence* between the larger index (S&P 500) and the sector itself. As you can see, I can tell a lot from this comparative line chart about how the sector is performing relative to the larger market.

> **Divergence** is the tendency for an individual stock or sector to move in a direction opposite to that of a larger index or the overall market.

Another of my favorite charts for intra-day trading is the three-minute chart. This is shown in Figure 5.2.

Here you see a more intense comparison between the same oil service sector (the line that rises over the charting period, traded with the symbol OSX.X) and the S&P. On the day that this snapshot was taken, would you say that the S&P had an uptrend, a downtrend, or no trend? Based on the very low volume demonstrated in the S&P line, it seems clear that there was no clear trend on that day. The S&P stayed in a trading range the entire day, without setting any higher highs or higher lows. It was just very, very flat.

FIGURE 5.2 - Oil Sector vs. S&P 500 Futures, 3 minute

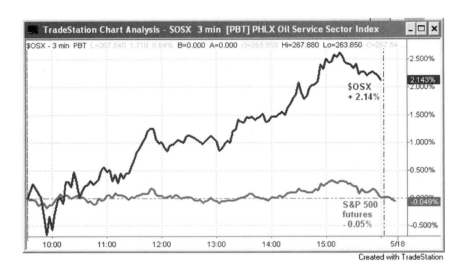

Source - TradeStation

Now take a look at the oil service sector line. The sector was clearly in a very strong uptrend on the same day. Had I not overlaid the two indices, how would I have known that? Would I have known that sector was an uptrend? I wouldn't have had any way to tell unless I had been watching a ticker carefully to see the percentage go up. You can do that, too. That's a more advanced way of doing this; but for beginners, I recommend that you use this simple overlay method.

Of course, hindsight is always perfect, and we can go through charts all day long, telling ourselves what happened; but how does this help you to know, in the moment, when to get into a sector during the course of its trend? That is a tougher question. You know the answer by checking the divergence between the sector and the broader index, in this case the S&P 500 Futures. The very first clue that this sector was strong was obvious to me by about 10:00 in the morning. At that point, I knew for certain that I wanted to be in this sector on this day.

Now think about the ramifications of observing a divergence as it occurs. If a sector is strong enough to rally even as the market is selling off, what do you think happens to that sector when the market reverses? It goes screaming higher. In the example shown in this chart (Figure 5.2), if the S&P had rallied at the end of the day, there was a very strong likelihood that the oil service sector would have continued upward even more strongly.

Why is this? If there are enough buyers in that sector to cause the sector to rally even as the market is selling off, then that's going to be the first sector to take off when the market turns. You will recall that one purpose to intelligent sector trading is to minimize your risks and maximize your profits. This oil service sector chart is a perfect example of this principle in action.

If you were long in this sector, even as the market was dropping, your risk would have been less than if you were in the entire market. Your risk would be less because this sector has demonstrated relative strength. If the market were to continue dropping, this sector would eventually drop also, but not point for point and not as drastically; the chart demonstrates this. Eventually the buyers throw in the towel, but this would be one of the last sectors to turn around and follow—and it probably wouldn't be a freefall. Instead, it would tend to stop setting new highs, slow down and move sideways, consolidate a little bit and then start to sell off, giving you plenty of time to get out. In comparison, a sector that's following the market and dropping just as hard as the market will bring you more grief, more rapidly.

The point I am making here is shown in the divergence of the chart between the S&P and the sector. As the S&P continued selling off and then settled into its flat period, the oil service sector kept setting new highs, one after the other, totally ignoring the market and contradicting what the broad indicator implied.

I have heard some technicians complain that this divergence analysis is not useful because you cannot tell whether a sector has relative strength until the end of the day. This is not the case. In the example, I knew by 10:00 a.m. that the sector had relative strength; it was a big red flag. I had to be in that sector on the long side because of the very early clue—the market selling off while the sector was rallying. This early signal was not isolated; the divergence continued the whole day and, in fact, became even more pronounced. The relative strength of the sector grew stronger as the market fell and then went flat.

Let me show you another example. Figure 5.3 shows a comparison for the oil service sector on a different day.

On this day, the oil service sector was weak. The reason for this weakness was a tech stock rally that afternoon. Once again, we saw an example of sector rotation, money going out of the old economy stocks, including the oil service sector, and into the technology

FIGURE 5.3 - Oil Sector, Relative Weakness

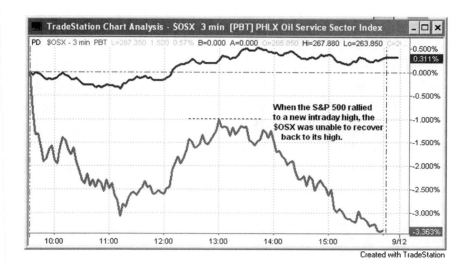

When the S&P 500 rallied to a new intraday high, the $OSX was unable to recover back to its high.

Source - TradeStation

stocks, so you could have actually shorted the oil service that day and bought tech stock sectors.

This chart shows you the exact opposite of what happened in the previous case: the reciprocal relationship between a sector and the broader market. Instead of a sector with relative strength, the oil service sector showed relative weakness on this day.

The S&P here wasn't really doing much of anything most of the morning. It was in a trading range up to that point; but then in the afternoon the S&P had a nice rally and went on to set about five or six higher highs throughout the rest of the session. During that time the S&P was setting higher highs, oil service could barely muster up or bounce off the lows of the day. It couldn't even bounce more than about one-third off its low price.

When you see that a sector is this weak, it is revealing. In this instance, we saw a huge rally going throughout the broader market, but the sector couldn't bounce more than a third off its low. In this case, I'd sell the sector short. Why? If the S&P were to sell off after its run-up on this day, what do you think would happen to that sector? It would set a new low just like the previous example in which the oil service sector set a new high on the first bounce of the S&P. If there were a market-wide sell-off here, you would see that the oil service sector would follow and would set a new low. That is a perfect condition in which to be short on that day.

You need to ask yourself: Do I want to short the sector in this condition? Even with this huge rally in the market, you wouldn't want to be short in that sector because rule number one is always trade with the trend of the market. In this case, the S&P was up, so you wouldn't want to be short, even in this sector. Your risk/reward ratio is going be stronger when you find a sector that's strong relative to the market versus a sector that's weak relative to the market. Don't get confused between a "strong trend" and an "upward trend." Remember, strength can include downward indicators. What I'm saying here is that you are usually better off going short on a sector whose downward trend relative to the market is strong rather than one that is weak.

Even so, you can make an argument favoring going short in some cases. As I said, you're better off in terms of risk/reward when

FIGURE 5.4 - Oil Sector, Short Opportunity

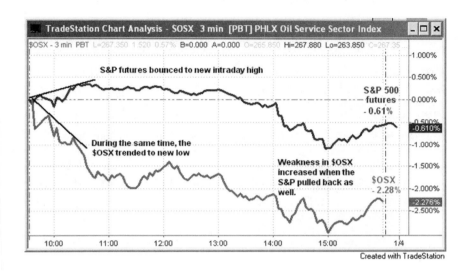

Source - TradeStation

working with strength rather than weakness. But there is a compelling argument countering this in some cases. Let's take a look at Figure 5.4.

My first clue that things were changing occurred when the S&P bounced from its lows all the way up to test the highs of the day, then rallied all the way back to the highs of the day. If the oil service sector had been strong, it should have also rallied back to test its high of the day; but instead, the sector just bounced off its lows. It couldn't even muster up that much of a bounce. That told me that if I wanted to go short on that sector it was a pretty good bet to do so because when the S&P formed its double top and started to come back down, that was a signal that the sector was going to fall off a cliff; and that's exactly what happened.

Now, the next question is: How do I determine which sectors are strong, and which sectors are weak? First, I set up a market minder on my trading software called "Sector Indices." These are the common sectors off our master stock sheet that I trade. A worksheet like the one I use is shown in Figure 5.5.

CEX, on the first row, is the chemical sector, which includes stocks like 3M and DuPont. The next line shows DJU, the Dow Utilities. If you look all the way to the bottom, you see SOX, which is the semi-conductor index.

This chart gives me my first clue about each sector's strength and weakness. This is my starting point when I'm trying to figure out what sectors are strong and what sectors are weak for the day. Notice how I have dynamically sorted the sectors by change in percentage on the day. They are not alphabetical.

The column labeled "Chg. %" is my percentage of change, the order for sorting the sectors. I have this set up to update continuously. As one sector gains strength, it's going to jump ahead; and as another sector loses, it moves down. On this particular day, I took the screen shot, and there wasn't a single sector that was up on the day. Out of all these sectors, the strongest one, in terms of changing percentage alone, was the chemical sector, CEX.

This doesn't mean that sector had relative strength. You can't just look at the tickers and say, "Semi's are down 4.7%, so they must be weak; I'm going to short them." You can't do that. But, it does give

FIGURE 5.5 - Sector Indices

SECTOR INDICES

	Symbol	Last	% Chg.	Low	High	Change
←	$CEX.X	404.76S	-.19	403.06	406.51	-.78
←	$DJU	338.77S	-.50	337.56	340.74	-1.69
←	$DRG.X	391.9 S	-.94	389.0	392.5	-3.7
←	$XNG.X	211.11S	-1.01	210.79	212.66	-2.16
→	$OSX.X	85.92 S	-1.20	85.35	86.86	-1.04
→	$IUX.X	723.13S	-1.33	719.32	729.18	-9.77
←	$DJT	2824.6?S	-1.38	2816.48	2864.91	-39.57
→	$BKX.X	888.53S	-1.41	884.98	895.95	-12.73
←	$XOI.X	551.27S	-1.50	550.15	555.31	-8.37
←	$RLX.X	869.35S	-1.52	862.74	870.64	-13.38
←	$XTC.X	863.77S	-2.20	860.57	868.72	-19.42
→	$BTK.X	492.78S	-2.68	492.67	503.33	-13.57
→	$NWX.X	296.92S	-2.85	294.28	299.89	-8.70
→	$HWI.X	153.92S	-3.18	152.88	155.14	-5.05
←	$GSO.X	165.60S	-3.27	165.22	167.90	-5.60
←	$TXX.X	528.44S	-3.27	526.82	534.91	-17.89
→	$IIX.X	144.21S	-4.43	143.98	148.14	-6.69
→	$SOX.X	555.54S	-4.72	552.41	564.31	-27.49

you a starting point. I can say, "It looks like the semi's are getting hit today, so I am going to overlay the CEX sector with the S&P and actually see if that is the case."

If the overlay shows that the sector is not only down 4.7% but that sector is also not able to rally with the market, then that confirms relative weakness. Remember, strength is relative to the market and not just to other sectors.

Next, I like to look at volume. If the sector's stocks are selling off in high volume, I want to short the Semi's. I never look at just the change in percentage and go short or go long based on that. The chart is only a starting point. It gives me an idea. Often you will see that sectors and the overall market mirror one another, so the relative strength or weakness is neutral. This is what I recommend you do—set up a market minder that has each of your sector indexes listed so you can look at it each day and sort it by change on percentage. This becomes your starting point.

Case Studies:

Let's illustrate some of these principles with a few case studies.

Sector Leader- Johnson and Johnson

Let's look at why you trade a leader and not the lagger. Remember that was one of our four keys. Johnson and Johnson, without even looking at our stalk sheet, is considered a leader of the drug sector. Why? Let's look at the basic criteria.

First off, we look at average daily volume. Typically the more volume that a stock trades within a sector, the more likely that stock is to be one of the leaders. J&J's average daily volume is about 13 million shares a day.

Next, market cap—generally the larger the market cap is of a particular stock, the more likely it is to be one of the leaders of that sector. Market capitalization of J&J is 167 billion.

Third would be liquidity. J&J's three billion shares means that it is a pretty liquid, pretty thick stock. But on a more basic level, you know who the leaders are by just being a consumer. Unless it is an industry you are unfamiliar with, you are going to be able to recognize the leaders because they are going to be your household names.

Let's look at Figure 5.6. On this particular day, notice that J&J had relative strength. It was in an uptrend the whole day. You see the lines here that I illustrated. That shows you J&J's uptrend. Ever since the morning it set a series of higher highs and higher lows from here all the way up to here. The lines of course indicate higher highs.

The S&P, on the other hand, did not break its high of the day until late. J&J from the time it opened immediately set a new high and by the time the S&P broke its high of the day, J&J had already set four new highs on the day. It's a fine distinction, but once your eye is trained to pick this information up, I would have known by J&J's second high that it is a relatively strong stock to be in. It also tells me that if the S&P turns, this sector is going to take off and, in this case, it does. Notice that J&J had relative strength all the way at the end of the day. Why? Because it's one of the leaders of that sector and your leaders are going to be your strongest stocks.

FIGURE 5.6 - Johnson & Johnson, Market Leader

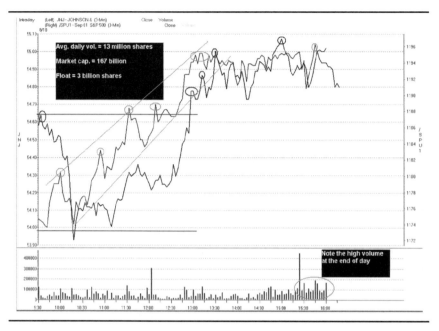

FIGURE 5.6 - Johnson & Johnson, Market Leader

Source - RealTick

Also, notice the high volume down at the end of the day. Volume is the momentum that keeps the stocks rallying. That's why that stock was able to consolidate at its highs even as the market sold off. Those are buyers that were stepping to hold that stock up even as the stock was selling off. This is a perfect example of a leader.

Sector Lagger: American Home Products (AHP)

Now that we've looked at a leader, it's time to review a lagger. Figure 5.7 is of AHP, American Home Products, on the same day; but,

FIGURE 5.7 - AHP, Market Lagger

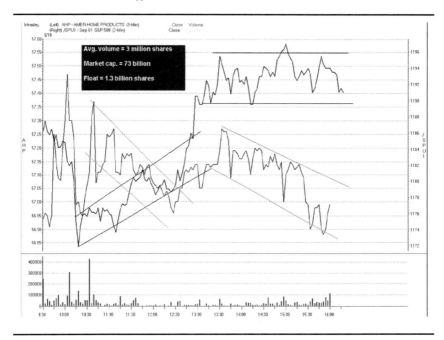

Intraday   (Left) AHP - AMER HOME PRODUCTS (3-Min)   Close Volume
(Right) /SPUI - Sep 01 S&P 500 (3-Min)   Close

Avg. volume = 3 million shares

Market cap. = 73 billion

Float = 1.3 billion shares

Source - RealTick

unlike J&J, it is not a market leader. Notice the chart of the S&P is the same, but the chart of the stock looks very different.

If we take a step back and review our criteria, we'll start to see the reasons why. The average volume of AHP is three million shares as opposed to J&J's thirteen million, meaning that J&J trades about four times as many shares on a given day. Market cap at AHP is 73 billion; J&J is about double that. The float (shares publicly owned and traded) is about 1.3 billion shares and J&J is almost triple that

FIGURE 5.8 - PTEN 15 Min

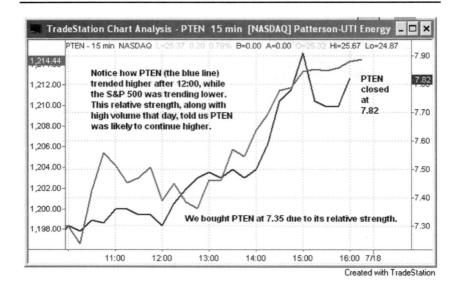

Notice how PTEN (the blue line) trended higher after 12:00, while the S&P 500 was trending lower. This relative strength, along with high volume that day, told us PTEN was likely to continue higher.

PTEN closed at 7.82

We bought PTEN at 7.35 due to its relative strength.

Created with TradeStation

Source - TradeStation

as well. Without even looking at a chart, we should know that AHP is not going to be a leading stock based on those numbers.

Even though this sector was rallying, was more money flowing into J&J or AHP? Obviously J&J because it's one of the leaders. If we were to look at Merck and Pfizer and Lilly and Bristol Myers, most likely their charts would look very similar to J&J on this day because those are the leaders of the sector.

Notice the trend lines—AHP was actually in a downtrend two times that day and ended up closing near its low of the day. While the S&P was rallying, AHP was selling off. This is why it is so important to trade leaders and not laggers in a strong sector. By the way, the volume of this stock was less than the average daily volume and J&J's was about 200% of its average daily volume. Again, money flow is your reason why.

High Volume: Patterson Energy

Our next chart, Patterson Energy, is an oil service stock (Figure 5.8). This is an example of a stock that's trading at a high volume. This particular day, we were long this stock, getting in on PTEN at $7.35 or so in the mid-morning session. The stock rallied to $7.82 for an almost 10% move in one day! Who says you can't make money trading oil stocks?

The S&P futures formed kind of a micro downtrend right during the same time that Patterson Energy, PTEN, broke a tie of the day and started rallying to new highs. As the S&P was going down, PTEN was going up.

Remember, if a sector doesn't sell off when the market does, that means when the market turns it's going to what? Go up. Well, look what happened. The S&P turned and the stock just took off.

High volume is the reason it could breakout like it did. If the chart looked like this, but the volume wasn't strong, I wouldn't have touched it. The volume convinced me that even if the S&P kept selling off, there would be enough buyers in there to lift the stock up.

To summarize, to trade sectors by relative strength, the first thing is to determine the trend of the markets. If the markets are in an uptrend, we look for sectors that are showing relative strength. On an intraday basis if the markets are on a downtrend, we look for sectors that are showing relative weakness to go short. Or you can do both if there's divergence.

> Remember, once you identify the sector you want to be in, you're going to trade the leaders, not the laggers and you are going to look for those that are trading on high volume or higher than average volume.

The next sections take our discussion into the next level, deciding which methods to use in employing your sector trading strategies. Several different modes can be used, and I have devoted one section to each.

Self-test questions

1. Candlestick charts are valuable analytical tools:

   a. when two or more sectors' candlesticks are reviewed together

   b. when a sector and overall market candlestick are overlaid

   c. in cases for singular analysis of a stock or sector, because overlaying two or more trends is difficult with the candlestick format

   d. for stocks and futures but not for larger sectors

2. Moving averages are useful tools in sector trading because they show:

   a. divergence between the long-term market trend and the sector

   b. the overall market averages without any sector movement factored in

   c. a likely path for stock or sector movement in the future

   d. the true volatility in a sector over time

3. Divergence is best applied between:

   a. two sectors operating on a reciprocal basis

   b. two sectors within the same old or new economy grouping

   c. the market and individual stocks, as a means for visualizing beta

   d. one sector and the broader market as measured by indices

4. Relative strength or weakness is most accurately measured between:

    a. volume and price
    b. two related sector trends
    c. morning and afternoon price trends
    d. a sector trend versus the market trend

5. Selling short is normally a wise strategy when:

    a. the sector is demonstrating relative weakness in a strongly up-trending market
    b. the sector is trading strongly, relative to the market's trend
    c. both sector and the overall market demonstrate weakness in an uptrend
    d. both sector and the overall market demonstrate strength in a downtrend

For answers, go to www.traderslibrary.com/TLEcorner

Chapter 6

Swing Trading on the Sector Level

In recent years, the evolution of *swing trading* has taken over the thinking among technical analysts. An expanded version of *day trading*, a swing trade usually takes between three and five days to complete. Technicians have come to recognize the strong and compelling advantages to be gained from following, identifying, and then trading at points where stock prices swing from one direction to the other.

When swing traders employ stocks, they may enter a position on either the long or short side; they can go long and buy shares of stock, or they can go short and sell shares of stock. In the basic theory of swing trading, it doesn't matter which direction you begin with, as long as you have identified the signals and know when to enter the trade.

The same distinctions and rules that work for single stocks can be applied to trading sectors as well. This can be done in one of two ways. First, you can swing trade using sector tracking stocks. Second, assuming that the leading stocks within a sector set the course for the other members of that sector, you can "play" a sector as a swing trade using just the leaders (for example, in the pharmaceutical sector, you can swing trade in Merck as a means for playing the sector and, most of the time, benefit from the sector-wide trend by using that leading stock).

Swing trading involves looking for the signals that tell you a price movement is about to change directions. In this regard, swing trading works much like sector trading. Decisions about timing of trades are based on the study of specific signals. Swing traders look for three specific signals that this is occurring and use them separately or together.

Three or More Days in One Direction

The most apparent signal that a price is about to change directions occurs when movement has been in one direction three days in a row. Using candlestick charts, this pattern requires that the movement occur over the three days and that each day's opening continues the direction established by the previous day's closing price.

Types of Traders

Position Trading: a relaxed style of trading in which traders are taken over a period of months to years. The position trader ideally identifies big price fluctuations or price breakouts over a relatively long time period.

Swing Trading: involves taking positions that last a few days or weeks. This style describes most active traders because it requires precision but not the minute by minute attention of day trading or scalping.

Day Trading: a type of trading in which all positions are closed by the end of the day (none are held overnight). This trading style attempts to profit from intraday price fluctuations and requires active management.

Scalp Trading: the most active form of trading that involves frequent buying and selling throughout the day. These types of traders trade large volume on the smallest intraday movements, with trades taking place over seconds or minutes. This is the most high-risk style.

Narrow Trading Day

The end of the short-term trend is signaled when the trading range narrows after at least a three-day movement. It can take longer, and often a trend does extend beyond three days; that's just the minimum. The narrow trading day works as the alarm bell, telling swing traders that the direction is about to reverse. For example, if a stock has been trading over a range of six points per day, does so consistently, and then suddenly narrows down to a two-point range, that is a signal that the price is about to reverse direction. On the candlestick, this is seen by a vertically smaller box following three or more days of a larger box size. A swing trade is initiated on the first point when the price moves in a direction opposite to the established trend.

Unusually High Volume in a Single Day

The confirming factor is estimating the time of change in a trend's direction and it occurs when an especially narrow trading day is accompanied by unusually high volume. This is seen in the candlestick by a horizontally wider box than on previous days. The high volume acts as a sign that buyers and sellers have "gathered" together at the price top or bottom in this extremely short trend and that the price is about to turn around and head in the opposite direction. The high volume is caused by a lot of trading and positioning at the conclusion of the three or more days' trading on the trend.

The *narrow trading range* is a clear signal of a turn in direction. Remembering that a trend can last longer than three days is most important to the swing trader. The usual three- to five-day range is only a general guideline; a trend can last longer, but the signal the swing trader seeks is that narrower-than-average range.

Narrow trading range is a reduction from the established norm in the point spread in which a stock is trading. Swing traders see the narrow trading range (also called the narrow range day) as a signal that the price direction is about to change.

A price trend, whether in a single stock or in a tracked sector, can only do three things. It can rise, fall, or remain flat. I have already explained the importance of divergence between a sector and the overall market. This rule continues to apply; but when you add the technical signals for making swing trades, you add to your arsenal of sector trading weapons. The combination of the sector signal-watching guidelines I have previously covered, and the chart-based trends swing traders use is a powerful combination. It can help you to improve the use of divergence analysis, for example, to vastly improve and confirm a trend you observe within a sector.

Swing traders recognize that an *uptrend* consists of two specific patterns in the way that price ranges develop. The three-part testing of trends consists of three or more days with prices moving in the same direction, the narrow trading range, and the high volume day. More explanation is needed for the price movement segment of this test. The price must conform to a specific pattern to clearly establish the trend. In an uptrend, the price is expected to set a series of progressively higher highs, offset by a series of progressively higher lows. The typical pattern looks like this:

higher high	higher lows
23 - 25	21 - 23
26 - 27	25 - 26
28 - 30	25 - 27
31 - 32	26 - 29

Prices can also move downward, but again, specific criteria must be met. A *downtrend* is defined as a series of progressively lower lows, offset by a series of progressively lower highs. For example, a downtrend is set when the following pattern emerges:

lower lows	lower highs
29 - 26	33 - 28
25 - 24	27 - 26
23 - 21	25 - 22
20 - 18	21 - 19

The third possible price pattern is the *sideways trend*, characterized by little or no movement beyond an established trading range with relatively equal high and low points. If you assign emotions to the various kinds of short-term trends, an uptrend would be greed, a downtrend fear, and a sideways trend uncertainty.

This indecision, in which neither buyers nor sellers are able to dominate the price trend, often occurs as a previously established price level slows down. This pattern becomes established in terms of trading range, degree of back-and-forth price movement, and volume. For example, the trading range settles into a flat support and resistance line rather than one with price movement; the level of price swings without this trading range narrows down; and volume also becomes consistent. The uncertainty of the sideways trend is characterized by these signs.

Swing trading can add a dimension to sector trading not otherwise available. As a rule, a sector trading analysis compares relative strength or weakness between the sector and the market, trading sector-tracking stocks or sector-leading stocks, and identifying points of divergence to signal buy and sell decisions. A swing trade analysis tends to focus on an individual stock. The use of swing trading may have the best application when (a) you begin with a study of divergence between the sector and the market, (b) you recognize the relative strength of the sector, and (c) you decide to open a position based on the combination of divergence, the relative strength, and the swing trading pattern, using a sector's leading stock as the vehicle for your sector/swing trade.

Swing trading within a sector strategy probably works best when you are playing the sectors by moving in and out of the sector leaders, since those are the stocks likely to establish the swing pattern. Once you find a good sector trade opportunity, you can move to the secondary swing trade analysis to seek confirmation. Because each sector consists of several stocks, the averaging effect of the overall sector might obscure the trends set by the leading stocks. The same argument applies to sector-tracking stocks (such as QQQ, SPY, and DIA for overall markets; and for BBH, PPH, SMH, SWH, TTH, WMH, HHH, and OIL for specific sectors).

A tracking stock is also an average of the entire sector. The danger in trying to use swing trading on these is going to be that actual strength or weakness of a trend in any one stock may be offset by opposite movement in another. If you want to swing trade your sector plays, I encourage you to employ the strategy only as a tool for timing sector leaders.

Anyone who enters into a sector trading strategy soon realizes that it's all a matter of timing, reading signals, and knowing how to interpret trends. Hindsight is great, and I wish there were some way to take a position on hindsight; but when you're in the middle of a trading day and things are evolving rapidly, it is much more complicated to make the right call at the right time.

Now imagine a different situation. If you track sectors and watch divergence trends, and then focus on sectors showing relative strength (including, of course, a clear leader), you can combine all of that information with five-day candlestick chart formations for the leading stocks of each industry. In fact, it is also possible to combine sector tracking with swing trading analysis on a single candlestick chart. You look for all of the indicators to click at the same moment on the sector's leader: relative strength, divergence between sector and market, and the swing trade signal. This multi-layered confirmation can only improve your percentages for sector trading profits.

The next section examines and compares the decision to take long and short positions and explains the levels of risk to each one.

Self-test questions

1. Swing trading is a strategy designed to:

   a. take advantage of back-and-forth trends between sectors

   b. move money from one sector to another based on relative strength

   c. enter trades at the beginning of price reversals and close them at the end

   d. offset long positions in stocks with short positions in sectors

2. Three specific signals are employed in swing trading. These are:

   a. price movement in one direction for three days or more, a widening trading range, and consistently strong trading volume

   b. price movement in one direction for three days or more, a narrowing trading range, and unusually high volume on the narrow trading-range day

   c. uncertainly in price direction, a widening trading range, and high trading volume

   d. uncertainty in price direction, a narrowing trading range, and low trading volume

3. A narrowing trading range tells swing traders that:

   a. the established trend of three or more days in the same direction is coming to an end and prices are going to begin moving in the opposite direction

   b. traders are becoming disinterested in the stock

   c. a large-scale breakout to the upside is about to begin

   d. the stock is not as reliable for sector trading as the broader sector

4. Uptrends and downtrends, respectively, are established by a pattern of:

   a. higher highs and higher lows versus lower lows and lower highs

   b. higher highs and higher lows versus higher lows and lower highs

   c higher highs and higher lows versus lower lows and higher highs

   d. higher highs and higher lows versus lower lows and lower highs

5. The use of swing trading within a sector trading strategy is best applied:

   a. using the entire sector

   b. using sector leaders

   c. using tracking stocks

   d. any of the above

For answers, go to www.traderslibrary.com/TLEcorner

Chapter 7

Buying Long and Selling Short

As with any trading strategy, before deciding how to proceed, you need to assess the risk. Both risk exposure and profit potential define strategies. Risk and profit potential also coexist and have to be understood as one aspect of a strategy.

The most basic way to trade sectors is through the *equity position* in a stock. In trading sectors, the most convenient way to take up an equity position is by trading shares of companies or tracking stocks. When you buy shares in a company, you own equity; and when you begin your transaction by *selling short*, you relinquish equity (and its obligations) to someone else.

Selling short is a strategy in which the sequence of events is sell-hold-buy instead of the better-known long position of buy-hold-sell.

A long position can be taken in a tracking stock or in a sector's leaders. I have already given you some examples of this. Rather than buying the pharmaceutical tracking stock, for example, you can go long by purchasing shares of Merck.

The risk in a long position is always that the stock will fall in value. No one wants to lose money in a stock investment, and this troubling possibility is always present when you buy shares. Because no one wants to realize their losses, there is an all too human tendency to *take profits* in stocks that appreciate in value and to wait out the market on those stocks that have lost value. As a consequence, many investors end up with a portfolio full of stocks valued below their basis. This accumulation of *paper losses* ties up capital and contradicts the purpose of trading, which, of course, is to make profits.

If you plan to sector trade on the long side, acquiring shares has to be understood in terms of both potential and risk. You want a fairly volatile stock because you're seeking short-term profits through sector trading. Volatility is characterized by a good degree of price movement, and you want to get in and out of positions quickly; but, volatility also equates to higher risk by its definition. A volatile stock is likely to be volatile in both directions; so, before you begin acquiring stocks as part of a sector trading strategy, it's important to remember that even with all of the signals in place, there are no guarantees.

To manage risks in a sector trade involving a single stock sector leader, you really do need to accept the possibility that the price will move in a direction you didn't plan. If and when that happens, you need to be prepared with a contingency plan.

You Are Willing to Acquire and Hold the Stock until the Price Trend Changes

In other words, you would be willing to acquire the stock at the current price even if your short-term sector strategy does not work every time. The problem with this contingency is that you are likely to tie up more capital than you intend to by holding depreciated stock.

You Enter a Stop-loss Order to Cut Losses Before They Become Too Extreme

In chess, good players tell you that when you lose the advantage, the smart thing to do is to retreat and go on the defense. Only an inexperienced player continues attacking in the hopes of getting even. Cutting your losses quickly frees up capital and lets you move on to the next trade.

You Minimize Your Capital Exposure

You certainly should not put more money into sector trading on the long side than you can afford; and I would advise most investors to avoid sector trading on margin.

Going short is the opposite of the long equity position, but the risks are substantially greater for a couple of reasons. When you go long, you own the shares, you accept a loss or hold indefinitely, and you wait for a price rebound; but when you sell short, the transaction is far more complex. First of all, your broker has to buy the shares for you and then lend them to you, so short sellers pay interest on those borrowed shares. Time works against short sellers because the interest accumulates as time goes by. Secondly, as a short seller, you hope that the share price falls so that you can buy and close at a price below your original sales price. To make a profit, you have to get enough of a point spread to cover the original cost, interest, and brokerage fees.

Short sellers can sector trade when they see relative strength in a sector leader on the downside. Combined with the signals used by swing traders, you can time your short sale based on three- to five-day signals that I covered in the previous section. I believe that combining swing trade timing with sector trading analysis provides you with the information you need to beat the averages, but there are no guarantees. I recommend short selling only for the most experienced traders. For everyone else, stay with the traditional long strategy of buy-hold-sell and leave the sell-hold-buy to those who are willing and able to take on greater risks.

I focus on leading stocks within sectors for actual share trades only to make the point that risk is a part of the equation. You can buy shares in tracking stocks, but price movement is going to represent an average for the sector. If the leader accounts for all of the relative strength, but some members of the sector are weak or moving in the opposite direction, the sector tracking stocks may show little movement in either direction. The value to diversification is also its weakness. With this in mind, one of the better sector trading plays is to track the entire sector against the market, looking for relative strength and divergence; when it comes time to place your trades, go with shares of the leader.

Another alternative, executing sector trading strategies with ETFs, opens up many doors to flexibility and liquidity. The ETF may be the perfect vehicle for even, active trading. I will explain why in the next section.

Self-test questions

1. A long position involves:

   a. buying shares of stock
   b. executing trades in the buy-hold-sell sequence
   c. taking up an equity position
   d. all of the above

2. A short position involves:

   a. buying stock from your broker instead of on the exchange
   b. borrowing stock from your broker, paying interest on the stock, and selling the shares on the exchange
   c. selling a short lot or a number of shares less than the round lot of 100 shares
   d. executing trades in a short period of time, usually under a complete trading day

3. Section leaders may be most appropriate for sector trading strategies because:

   a. leading stocks are most likely to lead the trend, whereas the overall sector will include offsetting movement by weaker stocks within the sector
   b. risks of using tracking stocks are too high
   c. there is never enough divergence in the overall sector to create profits
   d. all of the above

4. The problem with profit taking in a long portfolio is:

   a. the tax consequences erode all profits taken in under one year

   b. it results in a portfolio of stocks valued below purchase price, tying up capital

   c. brokerage fees are higher for selling trades than for buying trades

   d. you need net losses for the tax benefits, so taking losses makes more sense than taking profits

5. With the risks of equity positions in mind, contingency plans may involve:

   a. holding the stock until prices rebound

   b. using stop loss orders to mitigate losses

   c. diversifying capital and only taking up equity positions to the extent you can afford

   d. all of the above

For answers, go to www.traderslibrary.com/TLEcorner

Chapter 8
The Exchange Traded Fund (ETF) Approach

For decades, investors have used mutual funds to compound their earnings, diversify risks, and profit from professionally managed portfolios, but there has always been one small drawback—funds have not performed well universally, proving the value of professional management is not foolproof.

In addition, mutual fund shares have to be bought and sold through the management. The lack of ability to trade shares on an exchange like stocks has always made mutual funds limited and more awkward to trade ... until now.

The Exchange Traded Fund (ETF) solves all of these problems. The ETF is a mutual fund that trades just like a stock on the public exchange. You can buy and sell shares as conveniently as stocks and as quickly. The portfolio is identified in advance because every ETF has a specific characteristic to its *basket of stocks*.

ETFs are available on virtually any combination of stocks or indices you can imagine: commodities, international corporations, precious metals, indices (ishares), countries or regions, treasuries and other money market instruments, and, of course, market sectors.

You can trade ETFs in many of the same ways you trade stocks: long equity, short sales, and even trading options. Please refer to *Appendix B: Efficient ETF Executions* for more detailed information. You can also trade ETFs on margin. Because there is no portfolio decision-making (the portfolio is defined by what is in the basket of stocks and not by buy or sell decisions), management fees and costs are low compared to those of mutual funds. You will have to pay a commission to trade in shares of ETFs; but in today's competitive online discount brokerage world, those fees are not deal-killers.

In other words, ETFs make the world of mutual funds flexible but maintain the diversification of the fund. Closely related to ETFs are HOLDRS, an acronym that stands for HOLding Company Depositary ReceiptS (pronounced "holders"). These securities represent ownership in the common stock or American Depositary Receipts (ADRs) of specified companies in a particular industry, sector or group. Issued by Merrill Lynch, there are currently seventeen different HOLDRS; fifteen of them track specific market sectors or industries and the other two are broad-based market indexes. Figure 8.1 illustrates the fifteen sector HOLDRS (and

FIGURE 8.1 - HOLDRs

TICKER	DESCRIPTION	AVG. DAILY VOL.
SMH	Semiconductor HOLDRS	8.3 million shares
XLF	Financial Select SPDR	2.6 million shares
OIH	Oil Service HOLDRS	1.2 million shares
PPH	Pharmaceutical HOLDRS	608,000 shares
RTH	Retail HOLDRS	604,000 shares
SWH	Software HOLDRS	540,000 shares
TBH	Telebras HOLDRS	495,000 shares
BDH	Broadband HOLDRS	328,000 shares
UTH	Utilities HOLDRS	270,000 shares
TTH	Telecom HOLDRS	250,000 shares
IIH	Internet Infrastructure	212,000 shares
RKH	Regional Bank HOLDRS	124,000 shares
HHH	Internet HOLDRS	115,000 shares
IAH	Internet Architecture HOLDRS	107,000 shares
BHH	B2B Internet HOLDRS	99,000 shares
WMH	Wireless HOLDRS	57,000 shares

Source - The Wagner Daily

one Select Sector SPYDER) that I track on a daily basis. By trading the HOLDRS, you can participate in a wide array of market sectors, reduce risk through diversification, and save commission costs. Each of the HOLDRS in the table is sorted by its respective average daily volume:

The ETF, which is an *investment company* just like a mutual fund, has the important distinction of having removed all discretion from a management team. In fact, no management duties are required other than monitoring a computer screen and recording bank deposits and withdrawals. The "objective" of mutual funds is described in terms of investment outcome: conservative growth, income, or balanced return, for example. An ETF, on the other hand, has the single goal of achieving the same return as a specific market index, stock type, commodity, or sector.

The ETF is uniquely different from traditional mutual funds in that ETFs can issue shares in large blocks known as *creation units*, which are then marketed over exchanges and through brokerage accounts to individual investors. I like to think of this as being similar to a public offering of stock issued by a corporation.

The ETF does not sell shares directly like mutual funds; which is an advantage. It would be difficult and awkward to attempt to use mutual funds in any kind of day trading or swing trading activity. It is too cumbersome and time-consuming to complete purchase and sale. A short-lived mutual fund day trading movement a few years ago fizzled out for this very reason. The typical creation unit-based marketing of shares goes from the ETF to institutional buyers, who then split up the large-block unit and sell on the secondary market (brokerages). In this way, small investors can buy as few shares as they want without having to figure out how to finance a large block purchase. This system makes ETFs available to a broad spectrum of individual investors.

When you own ETF shares, you can sell them through the exchange for the current bid price, just like stocks. Like all mutual funds, ETFs issue a prospectus explaining how the portfolio is composed, what is included, as well as other policies, fees, and restrictions. If a prospectus is not given directly to an individual investor, a product description (a summary of the key provisions in the prospectus) is provided.

The flexibility of the ETF, combined with its predetermined portfolio, makes it an excellent vehicle for sector trading. HOLDRs may also serve the same purpose; while these are somewhat more advanced, they work on the same principle. If you want to sector trade with a broader portfolio than just the sector leader, the ETF could be the answer. Of course, it is impractical for anyone to buy shares of all the stocks within one sector, so the ETF solves that problem. The previous chapters describing divergence and relative strength or weakness can be easily observed on a sector-wide basis by tracking ETFs for a particular sector. Because they trade like stocks, you can also track price changes throughout the day, unlike traditional mutual fund listings, whose open and close NAV is usually the only available listing information.

It would not surprise me if the convenience of ETFs eventually outpaced investment dollars in traditional mutual funds, variable annuities, and unit investment trusts. ETFs just make sense in a world becoming more accustomed each day to online investing and instant trades. The ETF alternative is worth exploring and keeping on your "shelf of strategic possibilities."

With all of this being said, I continue to believe that mutual funds have both a good side and a bad side. The ETF solves one of the biggest problems with traditional funds—management. With a predetermined portfolio, no actual decisions have to be made, so a good plan cannot be ruined with poor management timing, or with fees. Of course, you replace management fees with fees charged by your broker, so there is still no free lunch. Perhaps a greater consideration involves the diversification itself. The ETF, like all funds, is a collection of similar stocks, such as individual sectors; you get the average performance of that grouping of stocks. While diversification is desirable, this can also be a problem.

For example, what happens if you invest in one sector-specific ETF? Some stocks will do quite well, but others will perform poorly. Your ETF return will be the average of the whole picture, and this is not always a good thing. For example, if we go back to my example of the pharmaceutical sector, I know that I can trade the entire sector including excellent company performance and some that will lag behind; but my return will only be the average. I might prefer to track the sector, time my sector trade using Merck or another leader, and avoid all of the average or below-average performers.

The ETF is one of many avenues you can use for sector trading. I think the problem of averaging combined with the trading costs might offset the advantages, but it is worth considering. By the way, many ETFs can be traded using options in place of trading actual shares. This is a viable choice as you will see in the next section where I explain an equally intriguing and flexible method for sector trading, combining liquidity with great leverage.

This final section explains how sector traders can employ options as their trading mechanism of choice.

Self-test questions

1. Exchange-traded funds (ETFs) are unlike mutual funds because they offer:

   a. trading over public exchanges, just like stocks
   b. long or short positions
   c. option trading
   d. all of the above

2. A "basket of stocks" refers to:

   a. all of the stocks within a single sector
   b. a group of stocks held in a traditional mutual fund portfolio
   c. a group of stocks held in an ETF
   d. sector stocks traded in an institutional portfolio

3. An "investment company" is:

   a. any company managing money for its clients
   b. a company that manages its own portfolio of investments
   c. a mutual fund or ETF
   d. an institutional investor

4. ETF shares are sold:

   a. directly to the public through individual accounts opened by each shareholder

   b. only to exchanges, where shares are traded on the open market

   c. through the sector-tracking stocks for each sector-specific ETF

   d. in the form of creation units to brokerage firms in large blocks, and from there to investors over public exchanges

5. Sectors can use ETFs:

   a. as a convenient method for short-term trading, both long and short

   b. primarily as a divergence test only, but not for actual buying or selling

   c. only to diversify a portfolio and provide long-term alternatives to short-term sector trading activity

   d. Only when they can afford to buy large blocks of 50,000 shares

For answers, go to www.traderslibrary.com/TLEcorner

Chapter 9
Sector Trading with Options

A final topic I want to cover for you involves options. Now, many people hear that word, and they just shut down. They think, "Options are high-risk, complicated, and difficult to trade."

Actually, whether or not these statements are true really depends on how you use options. Some strategies are actually profitable, low-risk, simple, and easy to trade. In fact, options can be traded as easily as any other venue on the public exchanges, but of course, you have to know what you are doing. Before anyone starts using options, he or she must understand all of the risk and strategic possibilities. Why include this topic here? The answer—options are quite well suited for short-term sector trading. Based on the starting assumption that you use all of the skills presented in this book and assuming you are able to get a working knowledge of the options market, these tools are perfect for sector trading.

An *option* is a contract without any tangible value. It gives both buyers and sellers certain rights to trade shares—without being required to actually buy or sell the shares themselves. This is significant. Options can provide you incredible *leverage* because each option contract (representing 100 shares) is going to trade for a very small fraction of the price of 100 shares of stock. Options open up the door of possibility and enable you to sector trade on a far greater variety than you can do in any other way. Please refer to *Appendix C: Options Basics* for more information.

> **Leverage** is putting a small amount of money to work to control a larger block of value. An option leverages money; it is a single contract that enables its owner to control 100 shares of stock without being required to buy those shares.

Options are incredible tools for sector trading. They reduce your exposure to risk because they are cheap compared to stocks. For example, take a look at Merck, which is the leading stock in pharmaceuticals. In April, 2006, Merck (MRK) was trading at about $34 per share. If you wanted to sector trade 100 shares, you would have to invest $3,400 plus brokerage fees. When you trade options, you can execute a sector trade for about $200—and make the identical profit. Furthermore, you can trade on the belief that the sector is going to rise or fall, based on the usual indicators, without having to risk either buying 100 shares or selling short.

This is all possible because options are cheap compared to stocks. This is true because every option has an *expiration date* at some point in the future. After that date, options become worth, anyone interested in waiting out price movement for the l time becomes a problem. Since sector trading is a short-ter you can use options to your advantage, timing your buy and sell decisions over a few days, and cut risks while leveraging your capital.

When you want to go short using stock, you have to go through the complexities of borrowing shares from your broker and then selling them. This is expensive and potentially risky. You can achieve the same profit opportunities using options, with much less risk. This is because there are two kinds of options. A *call* gives you the right (but not the obligation) to buy 100 shares of a specific stock by the expiration date. A *put* gives you the right (but again, not the obligation) to sell 100 shares of the stock.

Call is the option granting you the right, but not the obligation, to buy 100 shares of a specific stock.

Put is the option granting you the right, but not the obligation, to sell 100 shares of a specific stock.

That specific stock is called the *underlying security*, and every call or put relates specifically to that company and no others. Each option is a contract for 100 shares, so the cost of an option gives you those purchase or sell rights. That does not mean you have to buy or sell the shares to make a profit from sector trading. When the stocks move in the desired direction (up for calls and down for puts) the option becomes more valuable and can be sold at a profit. So while option values go up or down for the same reasons as stock, they cost much less.

Getting back to the example of Merck, the stock was worth about $34 per share in April, 2006. Let's assume that under some conditions, I might track the pharmaceutical sector and want to buy; under other conditions, I would want to sell. If I employ stocks, I need to invest $3,400 (to buy shares) or obligate myself to borrowing 100 shares from my broker and selling short, but I can also buy either a call or a put.

At the same time Merck was at $34 per share, I could have bought a May 32.50 call for $200 or a May 35 put for $115. This gave me a full month before expiration, which should be plenty of time for the sector (and Merck) to make the desired movement in price either way.

Now, you notice that both a month and a price are specified in describing these options. The month is the expiration – specifically, the third Friday in May. The price is called the *strike price*, which defines each option. That is the price at which a call owner could buy shares; so if the stock's price rises above the May 32.50, that call will be more valuable than if it drops down to $28 or $29 per share. The put May 35 is specifically identified with the 35 strike price, so a put owner can sell shares at that price. If the stock fell below $35 per share, the put would increase in value. The lower the stock price, the more valuable the put, because it gives you the right to sell stock at $35 per share no matter how low the price goes.

> **Strike price** is the fixed price at which option owners are allowed to buy (call) shares or sell (put) shares by exercising their option.

Options are also available on sector tracking stocks, and this raises a whole range of strategic possibilities. I am focusing on single-stock options and using the sector leader as an example because this is probably the most appealing strategy for most people. Trading in options on Merck as a play on the pharmaceutical sector is viable and sensible, given the choice of buying or selling 100 shares at a time.

You may also note that the examples I gave were of a call below the current price and a put above the current price. These are called *in the money* options. When the stock's price is higher than the call's strike price, it is in the money; and when it is lower than the call's strike price, it is *out of the money*. For puts, the opposite is true. I prefer using in the money options for sector trading because their value moves dollar for dollar with the stock. It tracks the stock exactly, so I can use them just like stocks, and not change my sector trading strategy.

When the status is in the money, the point-for-point tracking occurs because the *intrinsic value* of the option matches the in the money points. For example, if a stock is three points in the money, the option has three points, or $300 of intrinsic value. But when the option/stock relationship is out of the money, the option's price does not necessarily track the stock. All of the option value in this condition is *time value*, or the value based on time until expiration. The more time, the more time value.

> **Intrinsic value** is the portion of an option's value equal to the points in the money. This occurs whenever the stock's price is higher than the call's strike price or lower than the put's strike price.

In the money options are perfect for sector trading. They not only cost much less than the stock itself but their risks are lower as well. A primary risk in buying options is that they will expire before you sell them; but because sector trading is designed to work best in the short term, you can buy very cheap options and achieve the sector trading goals with plenty of time. Risk is also lower because you're only putting a small amount of capital out there. Consider the example of Merck. Instead of buying or borrowing 100 shares for $3,400, you could purchase either a call or a put for $200 or less.

The call is the equivalent of buying shares in terms of how and when your sector trade would be profitable. A put is also a long position, but it is the equivalent of selling short 100 shares of stock. You can also sell options, but the risks are far greater; and I don't advise it. For one thing, you don't need to. You can use calls when you anticipate upward movement in the stock or sector and puts when you expect the stock's price to fall. Selling options is a far bigger topic, which I don't need to go into here. As a sector trader, you're better off sticking with long positions, especially when you can use the put in place of selling short.

This whole strategic approach to sector trading opens up many more possibilities. For example, because options are so cheap compared to single stock or sector tracking stock prices, you have much greater flexibility using options. You can trade many sectors at the same time, for example, even when you have only a limited amount of capital. You can also use multiple options to expand your profits. Let's take another look at Merck. Let's say you think the sector is going to move upward and you want to trade the sector, specifically using Merck stock. You are willing to invest $3,400. This means you can buy 100 shares or stock, or 17 calls. If you're right and the stock does move up, this increases your profits 17 times. For example, a three point move looks like this:

Buying 100 shares of stock	Buying 17 calls
Purchase price $3,400	Purchase price $200 x 17
Latest price $3,700	Latest price $500 x 17
Profit $300	Profit $5,100

These comparisons are provided without accounting for brokerage and trading fees, of course, but the example makes the point. Your profits are much greater using options than using shares of stock.

Of course, there is much more to options. I've just given you the highlights here, but these devices are excellent tools for stretching your capital, reducing your risks, and expanding your profits. Before you jump in, though, you should learn more on the topic. A good starting point is to go to the web page for the Options Clearing Corporation (www.optionsclearing.com) and download the free publication, "Characteristics and Risks of Standardized Options," which has a link on the OCC home page. Also, refer to *Appendix C: Options Basics*.

Self-test questions

1. An option is a contract:

   a. allowing you to choose between a single stock or a sector tracking stock

   b. that becomes profitable only if the market value of stock rises

   c. has no tangible value but provides exceptional leverage of capital

   d. designed primarily to trade on a sector-wide basis but not in individual stocks

2. Calls and puts are accurately described as:

   a. options that provide you with the right to buy (call) 100 shares of a specific stock or to sell (put) 100 shares of a specified stock

   b. contracts requiring their purchasers to buy stock before expiration date

   c. options to buy (put) or sell (call) shares from other investors

   d. high-risk and exotic investments suitable only for those with exceptionally large portfolios

3. The underlying security is:

    a. the stocks within a sector on which options are available
    b. any stock or other device included in a sector tracking stock
    c. the stock on which options are bought and sold
    d. another name for various subordinate classes of stock issued by companies

4. The term "in the money" describes a condition in which:

    a. the stock's market price is higher than a call's strike price or lower than a put's strike price
    b. the stock's market price is lower than a call's strike price or higher than a put's strike price
    c. an investor has paper profits that have not yet been taken through closing of the position
    d. investors' portfolio values are greater than the amount held on margin

5. The sector trading advantage of using in the money options includes:

    a. the ability to escape risk altogether
    b. leverage of capital to increase profit potential with less market risk
    c. benefits that can be realized only by trading sector tracking stocks
    d. a two-part process in which those in the money options are swapped for more profitable out of the money options

For answers, go to www.traderslibrary.com/TLEcorner

Appendix A
Table 1: Example Breakdown of Sectors

While our sector classifications are ever-changing and evolving, our latest breakdown among sectors and sub-sectors for all the sectors that we watch is summarized in Table 1.

This chart gives you a good idea of how I see the market and, more specifically, the market for sector trading. I have previously mentioned that I view these stocks using both technical and fundamental indicators; this is crucial because together these define how a sector gets on the list and which stocks end up as tracking stocks within sectors and sub-sectors.

Sectors	Biotechs	Computer hardware	Computer software	Computer storage
	Top-tier heavyweights	PC hardware OEM's	Productivity	Fiber-channel (FC) equipment
	Genetic mapping research	Unix Workstations	eBusiness apps.	Storage hardware
	Cancer	Conglomerates	EDA – electronic design automation	Storage networking software
	Diabetes	Manufacturing	Development tools	Storage peripherals
	Heart Disease	Handheld Computing (PDA's)	Application management	
Sub-sectors	Neurology	Test hardware	Entertainment	
TECH STOCKS:	Infectious		Security	
	Pharmaceutical Processing		Enterprise database apps.	
			Manufacturing support	

Sectors	Internets	Networkers	Semis CPU's	Small caps Wireless
Sub-sectors	Mega ISP's	Enterprise networking equipment (switchers/routers)	Graphics-video	Cellular voice service providers
TECH STOCKS:	eCommerce		Mixed-signal datacomm plays	Wireless local area networks (LANs)
	Online advertising	Backbone routers	Mixed-signal	
	Infrastructure (web hosting, portals, multimedia)	Next-gen packet switching and mixing equip.	Mixed-signal + DSP conglomerates	
	B2B	Optical WAN/telco plays (OC-12+)	Semicustom logic	
		Cellular telephone	Memory	
		Cable modem hardware	Semi equipment	
			Superconductors	

Table 1: Example Breakdown of Sectors | 113

Sectors	Banks and financials	Brokers	Chemicals and precious metals	Drugs
Sub-sectors: OTHER MARKET SECTORS:	Consumer financial services Money center banks Regional banks Insurance companies	Traditional brokers Discount brokers	Chemical manufacturing Plastic and rubber Precious metals	Major drug companies Second tier

Sectors	Healthcare	Power, utilities	Oil companies	Retail	Telco service providers
Sub-sectors:	Healthcare equipment and supplies	Power sector (high beta)	Oil producers	Department/discount stores	ILEC's (incumbent)
OTHER MARKET SECTORS:	Healthcare facilities	Alternate energy	Oil service (drillers)	Grocery stores	Major IXC's (Inter-exchange carriers)
		Traditional utilities		Drug stores	CLEC's (competitive local exchange carriers)
				Electronics stores	Wireless service providers
				Apparel stores	
				Specialty stores	
				Home improvement	
				Consumer (non-cyclical)	

Table 1: Example Breakdown of Sectors | 115

Appendix B
Efficient ETF Executions

The most important thing I have learned for getting good ETF executions is to always follow each ETFs respective index and use it as the basis for making entry and exit trade decisions. For example, if I am trading BBH, the Biotech Index HOLDR, I will always follow and chart $BTK, which is the symbol for the Biotechnology Index. If I am trading SMH, the Semiconductor Index HOLDR, I follow $SOX, the symbol for the Semiconductor Index. If I trade QQQ, I follow $NDX. Get the idea?

I get a much better feel for the true direction of the sector by watching its respective index. Because each sector index is comprised of a more diverse group of underlying stocks than the respective ETF, it is more accurate to watch the index instead because it will trend even smoother than the ETF. The bigger the spread on the ETF, the more important this technique becomes because it gives me a better idea as to where to place my limit order to try to get filled. If I am trying to buy or sell short an ETF HOLDR that has a big spread, knowing the relative strength or weakness of its respective index tells me my chance of getting filled if I try to buy or sell short at a better limit price than the prevailing market. Although some of the ETF HOLDRs and Index Funds can be a bit too illiquid for day trading or scalping, they are excellent for the types of multiple-day swing trades that we focus on because getting perfect fills is not as crucial. Let's look at a real live example.

On August 22, one of the plays in my newsletter *The Wagner Daily* was to buy OIH (Oil Service HOLDR) if it triggered past a price of 54.80, which it did within the first 30 minutes of trading. As soon as it triggered, I noticed that the specialist widened the spread on OIH, which made it difficult to know at what price to place my limit order to buy. Wanting to be sure if the rally was for real, I quickly consulted a chart of $OSX, the symbol for the Oil Service Index. I immediately realized there was a lot of relative strength in the index because $OSX was consolidating at the high of the day as the broad market was selling off. Therefore, I felt much more comfortable simply paying the offer for OIH because I was confident it was going to go much higher, which it did. By the end of the day, we netted more than 2 points on the trade. However, if I didn't consult the $OSX chart first, I may have never entered OIH because I would not have been as comfortable with paying up due to the large spread.

Let's look at what might have happened if the opposite scenario had occurred. Suppose that OIH triggered at 54.80 and once again had a large spread. We once again consult the chart of $OSX, but this time notice that the Oil Service index has simply been in a sideways trading range, chopping around, and is not showing much strength. This would cause me to believe that the specialist is just trying to suck in buy orders so he can quickly drop his offer and cover his shares for a profit a few minutes later. If I saw that scenario, I would either wait for more confirmation before buying OIH or place a buy limit order closer to the bid price rather than paying the existing offer. In the event I did not get filled, just as well, because the sector would not really have been that strong anyway. I will gladly pay a higher price later for the increased chance of the trade going in my favor.

While the biggest benefit to following the indexes is in executing less liquid ETFs, I have also found a benefit to watching the respective indexes of even the most liquid ETFs, which are QQQ and SPY. Even though both of these ETFs typically trade with a one to two cent spread, I have found that watching the Nasdaq 100 (NDX) and S&P 500 (SPX) is very beneficial during times of choppiness in the markets because it prevents me from getting shaken out of an otherwise good trade. Here's why.

If you watch QQQ and SPY trade on a level 2 screen (which is not necessary if you are exclusively swing trading them), you will notice that both of these ETFs possess a high concentration of ECNs such as Island, REDI, and Instinet on both sides of the market. Although I won't get into more detail on ECNs here, the main thing I want to make you aware of is that the intraday scalpers and momentum traders will often cause crossed markets with the slightest movement in the market. For those of you who do not know what a crossed market is, in this case it means that the ECN bid will be higher than the specialist's best offer or the ECN offer will be lower than the specialist's best bid. When you see this type of price action, it can often cause you to panic and stop yourself out, even though the Nasdaq 100 futures or the S&P futures may have barely moved. However, if you are watching the actual Nasdaq and S&P indexes instead of the underlying ETFs, you will not be subject to the jumpiness of the ECN traders who often only make a difference of a few pennies anyway. Once you see the actual market index make a solid move, THEN you can make a better decision to take your profits or your stop without doing so prematurely.

The easiest way I have found to follow both the sector index and its respective ETF is to set up a series of charts on your trading software that look something like this.

Figure B:1 is a 5-minute intraday chart that overlays $OSX with OIH, which allows you to see how one is trading relative to the other. I prefer a basic line chart because it is easier to see convergence or divergence with a line chart. I do, however, use a candlestick chart when viewing only one stock or ETF at at time. I recommend you set up overlay charts with each index and HOLDR so that you can quickly view price divergences (which also illustrate ETF arbitrage opportunities. . .but that's a whole different story).

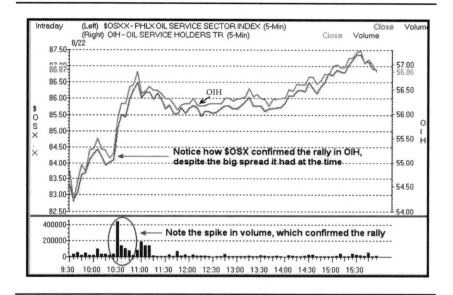

Source - The Wagner Daily

Here is a partial list of ETFs and their associated index symbols to get you started. You may need to check with your data provider regarding the format of the index symbol (some use a dollar sign, others don't):

ETF Symbol	Associated Index Symbol
QQQ	$NDX
SPY	$SPX
DIA	$INDU
SMH	$SOX

ETF Symbol	Associated Index Symbol
BBH	$BTK
OIH	$OSX
PPH	$DRG
SWH	$GSO
RTH	$RLX

Types of Orders and Optimal Routing

I have made the assumption that you have a brokerage firm who offers you a choice in how you route your order (primary market, third market, or an ECN such as Island). However, if you have a web broker who simply executes your order without the ability for you to choose the best route, there are still some ideas contained within that will assist you in getting better prices on your order fills.

Market or Limit?

As a general rule, I use market orders for executing both buy and sell orders. My philosophy on this is simple—it's better to get a bad fill and catch an 80 cent move in your direction than to miss getting filled by 5 cents and watch the trade go run 85 cents without you in it. Remember that I am typically looking to make 1 - 2 points of profit from most trades I enter and am usually in the trade for anywhere from 1 - 3 days. I don't trade with the intention of profiting from nickels and dimes, so I also don't worry about them when trying to get filled on an order. This is a lesson I have learned from my mistakes of the past when my insistence on getting a good fill continually caused me to miss substantial profits. I soon learned that being stubborn by using tight limit orders is not as profitable as simply trying to get an average-priced execution over the long-term. I know some traders will disagree with me, but this is what I have learned the hard way through years of personal experience and it is what works best for me. All that being said, there are indeed some instances when I do use limit orders on ETF trades.

The biggest factor that determines when I use limit orders is the liquidity of the actual ETF because some trade with much tighter spreads than others. In general, the more liquid a particular ETF is, the more likely I am to use a market order. Since high liquidity ETFs generally trade with a spread of only one to five cents, I usually get good fills with market orders and don't have to worry about chasing the price for pennies. However, when an ETF is illiquid, the spread will typically widen in correlation with the reduced liquidity. In those cases, I prefer to use a limit order. There are presently 21 ETFs that trade an average daily volume of 300,000 shares or more, which constitutes the entire realm of securities that I trade. However, there are 10 that I frequently trade. The list below shows whether I usually use market or limit orders on those 10 ETFs. There are always exceptions, but this list constitutes the type of order that I use a majority of the time:

Market Order	Limit Order
QQQ	BBH
SPY	OIH
DIA	PPH
SMH	RTH
	MDY
	XLF

With the less liquid ETFs that I have listed above, I have found the best strategy is to place your order either slightly above or below the middle of the spread, depending on whether you are trying to buy or sell. If I am buying, I place my order about 5 cents above the middle of the spread and place it 5 cents below the middle of the spread if selling or selling short (remember there is no uptick rule). For example, let's assume I am trying to buy BBH when the best bid is 83.20 and the best offer is 83.80. Assuming it is not a fast-moving market, I would probably place my limit buy order around 83.55. However, in a fast-moving market, I would place my order a little higher, maybe even go with a market order if I felt confident it was about to run a few points. Remember my goal is not to catch every single cent of a move, but just to catch a good piece of the move with minimal risk.

Order Routing

There are basically two choices with regard to how to get your order filled. The first choice is through a stock exchange such as the American Stock Exchange (AMEX) or the New York Stock Exchange (NYSE). The other option is to place your order through an ECN (Electronic Communications Network). For those of you who don't know, an ECN is simply an electronic network of computers that allows traders to trade directly with one another instead of via a stock exchange. This results in faster, and usually cheaper, order executions. The ECNs that trade the most ETF volume are ISLD, REDIbook, and Instinet.

Because of the speed of execution, I generally prefer to use an ECN for order execution. If I am trading QQQ, SPY, or DIA, I usually execute on Island. In fact, Island is rapidly becoming the standard execution choice for most traders who trade any of the ETFs. As of the time of this writing, Island trades 36% of the average daily volume in QQQ. This represents more than the combined percentage of both the NYSE and the AMEX! Island also executes approximately 33% of DIA volume and 25% of SPY volume. Although ECNs offer the fastest and most reliable method of execution, I have learned that there are times when executing your order through the AMEX is more profitable than through an ECN such as Island.

When an ETF has been trending all day and it suddenly reverses direction, you will notice that the inside market for Island and the other ECNs rapidly changes. However, due to the slowness of the specialist system, it often takes the specialist longer to update his inside market prices than it does with an ECN. You can use this lack of speed to your advantage if you need to get out of the position by immediately placing a market order to close your position.

Although there are going to be times when you occasionally get a bad order fill, I have found that I usually get a better fill through this method than if I would have joined the inside market on an ECN. More importantly, I am assured of getting out of the position. The most recent example of this happened to me when I was short SPY before a big morning reversal. As soon as the S&P Futures spiked up, traders on ISLD immediately jumped above the inside offer of the AMEX, creating a crossed market. I knew that if I executed on Island, I would have paid up quite a bit. So, I placed a market order to buy on AMEX and got filled at a price that was at least 10 cents better than what I would have paid if I executed through Island. This has happened to me on many occasions, but primarily it happens as soon as a market has reversed directions and the ECN traders have created a crossed market.

On a final note for those of you that have access to Level II quotes, I strongly recommend setting your Level II box to highlight the AMEX, as opposed to NYSE because AMEX typically leads the market with most ETFs. You will often notice that the third party exchanges such as BSE, CIN, PHS, CBO, and NAS are slow to update their quotes and often will show an inside market price better than AMEX or NYSE. However, you will rarely get filled at those prices. Although NYSE is the big daddy in the world of stocks, I have found they are rarely on the inside market of most ETFs. Instead, AMEX leads the inside market because ETFs are issued on the AMEX. Therefore, with regard to the two biggest exchanges, you will typically get a better and faster fill with AMEX than through NYSE when it comes to executing ETFs. Bear in mind, however, the exact opposite is true when executing a traditional stock of just one company.

Appendix C

OPTIONS BASICS

If you're a bit rusty on the basics and would like a modest refresher course on options, simply keep reading. What follows is a highly condensed primer describing what options are, how they work, general pricing guidelines, and some comments about elementary strategies.

Though options have been around in one form or another for several centuries, the modern era of options trading didn't begin until 1973, when standardized equity options were first introduced by the Chicago Board Options Exchange (CBOE). At that time, contracts were available on less than three dozen stocks, and trading was conducted in crowded pits by shouting floor brokers using hand signals and paper confirmation slips. Today, standardized options are available on more than 1,000 stocks, indexes, currencies, futures, and other vehicles; nearly 5 million equity options trade on an average market day. Well over 90 percent of those transactions are done electronically, with orders matched by computer and trades completed in a matter of seconds.

In other words, thanks to increased experience, improved computer technology, and electronic market systems, option trading has become fast, efficient, and relatively low cost—even for individual investors. But for those who've had only limited exposure to options and the arenas in which they trade, we'll review some of the basics.

What exactly is an option? Though there are a few variations, the basic definition is this:

An option is a contract giving the buyer the right, but not the obligation, to buy or sell an underlying asset at a specific price on or before a certain date. An option is a security, just like a stock or bond, and constitutes a binding contract with strictly defined terms and properties.

As securities, options fall into a class known as derivatives. A derivative is a financial instrument that derives its value from the value of some other financial instrument or variable. For example, a stock option is a derivative because it derives its value from the value of a specific stock. An index option is a derivative because it derives its value from its relationship to the value of a specific market index, such as the S&P 500. The instrument from which a derivative derives its value is known as its underlier or underlying asset.

By contrast, we might speak of primary instruments, though the term "cash instruments" is more common. A cash instrument is a security or index whose value is determined directly by markets. Stocks, commodities, currencies, and bonds all are cash instruments.

Regardless of what the underlying instrument is, there is one absolute regarding options: there are only two basic types (or classes). They are:

CALLS—A call option gives its owner the right to BUY the underlying security at a specific price for a limited period of time. In the case of equity options, the purchaser of a call receives the right to buy 100 shares of the underlying stock at the option's stated strike price. As a rule, purchasers of call options are bullish, expecting the underlying stock's price to rise in the period leading up to the option's specified expiration date. Conversely, sellers of calls are usually bearish, expecting the price of the underlying stock to fall—or, at the least, remain stable—prior to the option's expiration. However, there may be other reasons for selling calls, such as the structuring of strategies like spreads.

PUTS—A put option gives its owner the right to SELL the underlying security at a specific price for a limited period of time. With equity options, the purchaser of a put receives the right to sell 100 shares of the underlying stock at the option's stated strike price. Buyers of put options generally are bearish, expecting the price of the underlying stock to fall prior to the option's stated expiration date. Conversely, sellers of puts usually are bullish, expecting the price of the underlying stock to rise—or at least remain stable—through the option's expiration date. However, there might be other reasons for selling puts based on the objectives of certain strategies, such as lowering the cost basis on an intended eventual purchase of the underlying stock.

As the previous descriptions should make obvious, there are certain terms unique to options—terms that primarily describe the specifics of each individual option contract. To define these terms, let's assume you just bought a January 55 J.C. Penney Company call option at a price of $4.50.

- The underlying stock (or index)—This is the security that the option gives you the right to buy or sell. In this case, 100 shares of J.C. Penney Company, Inc. common stock.

- The strike price (also called exercise price)—This is the guaranteed price at which you can "exercise" your option (the price at which you can buy or sell the underlying stock). In this case, the price at which you can buy 100 shares of J.C. Penney stock is $55 per share.

- The expiration date—This is the date when your option expires (the date after which you can no longer buy or sell the underlying stock at the strike price). Options on stocks in the U.S. officially expire on the Saturday following the third Friday of the expiration month (although trading stops at the market close on the third Friday). Thus, this J.C. Penney call would expire on the third Saturday in January.

- The premium—The premium is simply the price you pay to buy an option, quoted on a per share basis. (The seller of an option gets to keep the premium, regardless of whether the option is ever exercised.) In this case, the premium was $4.50 per share, or $450 for the entire 100-share option contract.

Although they are traded as separate and unique securities, the essence of every option lies in its underlying asset, be it 100 shares of common stock, a leading market index, a foreign currency, a commodity futures contract, or any other item of value.

The importance of this link cannot be overstated if you hope to be successful as an options trader. That's because the characteristics of the underlying security will determine both the premium you pay (or receive) for the options you trade and the odds of your success with the strategies you choose. For example, assume you've been following a stock that has traded in a range of, say, $35 to $39 per share over the past six months. Obviously, options on that stock would be poor candidates for a strategy requiring either a $5-per-share price move or a rise above $40. And, if you wanted to sell options on that stock, you'd be unlikely to get premiums high enough to make many strategies worthwhile. (The example below discusses how option premiums are determined.)

Likewise, if you were interested in doing a stable-market option strategy, your odds of success would be very low if you tried it on a highly volatile market index or on a stock that had traded in a range from, say, $35 to $75 during the past six months.

Key Elements of an Option Premium

The price a buyer pays when he purchases an option—or receives when he sells one—is known as the premium. The buyer must pay the full premium at the time of the purchase (option premiums are not marginable), and the seller gets to keep it regardless of whether the option is subsequently exercised.

Equity option premiums are quoted on a per-share basis. Thus, a quoted premium of $3.75 represents an actual payment of $375 on a standard 100-share stock option contract.

The actual size of the premium for any given option is determined by a number of factors—but, in non-mathematical terms, the three most important are:

- The strike price of the option relative to the actual price of the underlying asset, which is known as the intrinsic value.
- The length of time remaining prior to the option's expiration date, which determines what is called the time value.
- The degree to which the price of the underlying asset fluctuates, referred to as the volatility value.

A basic, non-mathematical formula for option pricing could thus be:

> Intrinsic Value + Time Value + Volatility
> Value = Option Premium

Unfortunately, the only absolute in that equation is the intrinsic value. To illustrate, assume QRS stock was trading at $48 per share and you purchased a November QRS call with a $45 strike price, paying a premium of $5.50 per share. The intrinsic value of the call would be $3.00 a share—always the difference between the actual stock price and the call's strike price. (By contrast, a $50 call would have no intrinsic value because its strike price would be above the actual stock price, while a $50 put would have an intrinsic value of $2.00 per share—again, the difference between strike price and actual stock price.)

The remaining $2.50 of the $5.50 call premium would be attributed to a combination of time value and volatility value. There's no simple way to determine an exact breakdown of the two—though there are complicated mathematical formulas, typically using the Black-Scholes option-pricing model or variations thereof. As a refresher, two basics apply:

1.   The more time remaining until the option's expiration, the greater the time value portion of the premium.

2.   The greater the volatility of the underlying asset, the higher the volatility portion of the premium. Thus, in our November QRS example, time value would likely dominate the non-intrinsic portion of the premium in August, while volatility value would be a greater consideration in early November, after most of the time value had eroded.

Your Goals Help Determine Your Choice of Strategies

As noted earlier, options are among the most versatile of investment vehicles. They can be used for the most aggressive of speculations—and for purely defensive purposes. They can be used to produce large one-time profits, or to generate a steady stream of income. They can be used in the riskiest of investment pursuits, or specifically to insure against risk. They can be used when markets rise, when they fall, or when they fail to move at all. They can be used by themselves, in conjunction with other options of the same or different type, in combination with their underlying securities—even with groups of essentially unrelated stocks.

In fact, there are at least a score of distinct investment strategies using options alone—and another dozen or so using options in association with other securities or underlying assets. So, how do you select the right strategy?

Obviously, the goals you hope to achieve using options will dictate the strategies you employ. If you expect a major market move and your desire is to reap maximum speculative profits, then you'll likely pick the simplest and most direct of the option strategies: the outright purchase of a put or call, depending on your views about the direction of the move.

If you expect a more modest price move but still want to seek speculative profits, then you might take a more conservative approach, choosing a vertical spread using either puts or calls, again depending on whether you are bullish or bearish. If you expect a major price move but aren't sure about the direction, you may opt to position one of the more exotic strategies, such as a straddle or strangle. If you own a stock and need to generate more income from your holdings, you might add an option to the mix and write a covered call. Or, if you own a large selection of stocks and want to protect yourself against a market downturn, you could choose to buy puts on a broad-based stock index.

In short, the strategic possibilities—like the potential profits offered by options—are virtually unlimited. Whatever your specific goal, you likely can find a way to achieve it using options—assuming, of course, you are correct in your assessment of what the underlying market is going to do and that you structure your option strategy properly.

The following section discusses one element that can have a major impact on your strategy's success—choice of striking price.

Strike Price Positions & Strategic Risks

The choice of option strike price relative to the underlying stock price is a significant consideration when deciding exactly how speculative you want to be in buying options:

CONSERVATIVE—As a rule, the purchase of an in-the-money option represents the most modest speculation. Although it carries the largest premium, and is therefore most expensive in absolute-dollar terms, the in-the-money option actually is less risky because it requires the smallest stock price move to reach the break-even point and begin producing a profit. The stock also must make a sizeable move against you—enough to carry the option out of the money—before you suffer a total loss. On comparably sized price moves, real-dollar profits are larger on in-the-money options than on at-or out-of-the-money options. However, because of the higher cost, the percentage return on a profitable trade usually is lower.

MODERATE—The at-the-money option purchase provides the most balanced speculative play. The cost, and therefore the maximum risk, is moderate—as is the size of the stock-price move required to reach the break-even point and begin producing a profit. However, any adverse price move—or even a stable market—typically will result in the option expiring worthless, giving you a total loss. Dollar profits generally aren't as large, but percentage returns are higher than with in-the-money options.

AGGRESSIVE—The most blatant speculative purchase utilizes the out-of-the-money option. Although the premium, and thus the real-dollar risk, is low, the stock can move almost a full strike-price level in your favor—and you'll still suffer a total loss. And, an even larger move is needed before the trade starts making a profit. But, because of the small dollar outlay, when you do get one right, the percentage returns are quite spectacular.

Exit Strategies and Money Management with Options

Regardless of the option strategy you use, one rule always applies: Any time you implement a new trade, immediately plan an appropriate exit strategy.

This means setting both a specific loss limit and an anticipated target profit for every trade you do. It also means designating those benchmarks based on solid reasoning and sound market logic—not raw emotion. If you dislike such firm guidelines and start looking for ways to work around them, you're almost certainly headed for eventual trading failure, if not outright financial disaster. And remember, while you can give your profit targets some flexibility to allow for the pursuit of added gains, your loss limits should be absolute!

Another issue you should address in any options trading program is money management. Failure to properly apportion and control your capital can cause severe disruption—or even termination—of your trading program, regardless of the investments involved. However, with options or any other high-risk trading vehicle, a lack of clear goals and precise strategic objectives can spell disaster. Here are some of the most common mistakes you should strive to avoid:

- Trading based on emotion rather than on fact, which can lead to irrational or panic-driven decisions—and potentially devastating losses.

- Trading too much, thereby reducing the quality of your positions and increasing transaction costs.

- Initiating trades for which you're not mentally suited—that is, trades that keep you awake at night.

- Using strategies you really don't understand—then being surprised by the unanticipated outcome.

- Taking profits too soon—and holding your losing trades too long. With respect to the latter mistake, you should never be afraid to take a loss. Even the most successful option pros don't make money on every trade. So be willing to get out of a bad trade as soon as you recognize it. That's the first step in finding the next good opportunity.

- Losing too much too soon on too few trades, thereby leaving yourself with insufficient capital to make a later recovery.

- Taking advice from the wrong people, including the talking heads on TV who have an instant analysis for every minor market move.

Fortunately, if you start out with a solid plan, then do your homework before (and during) each of your trades, you can avoid most of these mistakes and develop into a competent—and successful—trader.

That covers the basic elements of options and the various ways they are traded, plus some fundamental tenets regarding risk and money management. Obviously, the information here is just the tip of the options iceberg. Far more sophisticated theoretical level in the body of this book.

Leading U.S. Exchanges

If you're going to be an active options trader, it's probably a good idea to know who's handling your orders—and your money. Although nearly 95 percent of options trades now are completed electronically, the leading options markets in North America still have distinct identities and a physical presence—the exception being the International Securities Exchange (ISE), the nation's first totally electronic options marketplace. Here is a brief overview of the five major U.S. option-trading arenas:

- Chicago Board Options Exchange (CBOE)—The CBOE originated the trading of listed options in the United States, introducing a slate of standardized call options on just 16 underlying stocks in April 1973 (listed put options didn't come along until 1977). Currently, the CBOE lists options on more than 700 stocks, bonds, and market indexes and boasts an average daily trading volume of more than 1.25 million contracts. The CBOE accounted for 35.6 percent of all U.S. option trades in 2004—a total of 320 million contracts—more than 95 percent of which were completed electronically.

- American Stock Exchange (AMEX)—The AMEX, based in New York, was organized to handle the trading of stocks too small to be listed on the New York Stock Exchange. It expanded into options soon after the CBOE introduced listed contracts and now accounts for about 14 percent of U.S. options trading volume. The AMEX allows trading in more than 1,400 different options, including those listed on all other major exchanges.

- Pacific Exchange (PCX)—The Pacific Exchange is the third most active options exchange in the world, trading options on more than 800 individual stocks and a number of indexes. The PCX is a leader in electronic options trading, handling roughly 95 percent of its trades electronically—72 percent of which are processed automatically, with orders typically filled in under five seconds. Based in San Francisco, the PCX options exchange accounted for nearly 15 percent of U.S. options volume in 2004.

- Philadelphia Stock Exchange (PHLX)—The PHLX was America's first organized stock exchange, founded in 1790, and remains a highly active trading arena. More than 2,200 stocks, 900 equity options, 10 index options and 100 currency options trade on the PHLX, which handles around 6.2 percent of U.S. options volume.

- International Securities Exchange (ISE)—The ISE has experienced overwhelming growth since its founding in 1997. Though it started slowly, with just 1 percent of the nation's trading volume in 2000, it has since exploded and now handles about 30 percent of U.S. option trades. Its interlinked computer network can provide up to 1 million quotes per second and is capable of matching buy and sell orders and confirming completed trades in five seconds or less.

Note: Options are also traded on the Montreal Stock Exchange, the Toronto Stock Exchange, and the Canadian Venture Exchange (in Vancouver), but listings are primarily for Canadian stocks.

Glossary

Basket of stocks refers to the portfolio of the ETF. It is determined by definition of the specific ETF and changes only if the underlying range (sector, for example) changes.

Breakout occurs whenever a stock's price moves above or below a previously established trading range.

Call is the option granting you the right, but not the obligation, to buy 100 shares of a specific stock.

Candlestick charts are valuable technical tools showing a stock's daily high and low prices, trading range, direction of movement, opening and closing price, and volume.

Capitalization ratio is any ratio that compares equity and debt sources of capitalization. Equity capitalization is the stockholder's equity (capital stock and retained earnings); and debt capitalization is the company's long-term debt (bonds and notes).

Chartist is a technician who predicts short-term price movement based on patterns found in a stock's price chart.

Creation units are large blocks of shares issued by ETFs for sale to the public through brokerage accounts on public exchanges.

Current ratio is a comparison between current assets (cash and liquid assets) and current liabilities (payable over the next 12 months). A standard expectation is a 2 to 1 current ratio (two dollars of assets for every dollar of debt).

Day trading is a strategy in which investors trade on extremely short-term trends within a stock, usually opening and closing a position within one trading day.

Debt ratio is a percentage derived to demonstrate the level of a company's dependence on debt versus equity. The total of long-term debts is divided by the sum of long-term debts plus stockholders' equity to find this ratio.

Divergence is the tendency for an individual stock or sector to move in a direction opposite of a larger index or the overall market.

Downtrend is the name assigned to a specific price pattern. It consists of a series of lower lows, offset by a series of lower highs.

Equity position refers to ownership of shares in a corporation. When you purchase shares, you are long in equity; and when you sell short, you have granted equity rights to someone else.

Exchange Traded Fund (ETF) is a type of mutual fund with a predetermined portfolio, which trades directly between investors and exchange (through brokerage services), just like stocks. ETFs also can be sold short and options can be written on ETFs.

Expiration date is the date options become worthless. All trades have to be placed for execution before that date.

Fundamental indicators focus on the financial results and status of corporations. Indicators relate to cash flow and valuation, capitalization, and profitability.

Head and shoulders is a popular price pattern consisting of two price plateaus (shoulders) and one higher plateau in between; or in the inverse pattern, a price level lower than the shoulder plateaus.

Holding Company Depositary Receipts (HOLDR's) are trust-issued beneficial ownership shares that can trade in market sectors.

In the money is the condition in which a stock trades above a call's strike price or below a put's strike price.Movement of the option's value tracks the stock dollar for dollar when in the money.

Intrinsic value is the portion of an option's value equal to the points in the money. This occurs whenever the stock's price is higher than the call's strike price or lower than the put's strike price.

Investment company is the legal designation for mutual funds, both traditional and ETFs.

Leverage is putting a small amount of money to work to control a larger block of value. An option leverages money: it is a single contract that enables its owner to control 100 shares of stock without being required to buy those shares.

Moving averages are technical tools showing how stock price movements are occurring over periods of time. Popular examples are 50- and 200-day moving-average charting tools.

Narrow trading range is a reduction from the established norm in the point spread in which a stock is trading. Swing traders see the narrow trading range (also called the narrow range day) as a signal that the price direction is about to change.

Net return is a percentage of profits to total revenues.

New economy refers, in a broad sense, to the tech stocks. These companies provide products and services that did not even exist fifty years ago and that are not always necessities. Demand tends to change cyclically for these stocks.

Old economy is, broadly speaking, a set of companies that have been around for a long time and that offer products that will always be in demand.

Option is the name of contracts providing buyers and sellers with contractual rights, including the right to buy or sell stock without needing to actually own shares. Each option relates to and provides rights for 100 shares of a specific, named stock.

Out of the money is the condition in which a stock trades below a call's strike price or above a put's strike price. Movement of the option's value does not track the stock's price but tends to decline as expiration approaches.

Paper losses are losses in share value of shares in a trader's portfolio. They become actual losses only if and when stock is sold.

Profitability ratio is any test of a company's ability to create, maintain and improve its operations and reported profits.

Put is the option granting you the right, but not the obligation, to sell 100 shares of a specific stock.

Realm of stocks is the approximately 300 companies trading in specific, identified sectors providing investors with the greatest potential for profits.

Resistance level is the top price of the trading range, or the highest price that buyers are willing to pay to acquire shares.

Risk-reward ratio is the inescapable connection between potential loss and potential profit. The higher the risk, the greater the opportunity, and vice versa.

Sector is the name given to a division of the market: a grouping of companies in the same industry, sharing the same or similar market and competitive factors, and subject to the same supply and demand and business cycles.

Selling short is a strategy in which the sequence of events is sell-hold-buy instead of the better-known long position of buy-hold-sell.

Sideways trend is a price trend in which neither an uptrend nor a downtrend have been established and which may represent a pause before price movement begins again.

Strike price is the fixed price at which option owners are allowed to buy (call) shares or sell (put) shares by exercising their option.

Sub-sectors are broken-down segments of larger, broader sectors, into intra-industry specialties for the purpose of defining sectors at a manageable level.

Support level is the lowest price, or the bottom of the trading range; the lowest price that sellers are willing to accept to give up shares.

Swing trading is the short-term execution of a trade, including opening and closing a position, usually within a three- to five-day time frame. It is intended as a means for identifying points where price movement is about to reverse from an established pattern and move in the opposite direction.

Take profits refers to the action of selling stocks as soon as they appreciate in value to obtain actual dollar value from appreciation and to avoid losses if and when market price declines.

Technical indicators are all indicators studying price trends of stock and studying price/volume combinations to anticipate price movement.

Time value is all of an option's value except intrinsic value. Out of the money options consist entirely of time value.

Tracking stock is the stock that leads a sector or sub-sector. Identification is crucial because the tracking stock tends to lead the rest of the sector in price trends.

Trading range is the area between established high and low trading prices of a stock. The range indicates the degree of volatility, or "breadth" of trading, and provides a distinction between low- and high-volatility stocks.

Underlying security is the stock options refer to. Calls and puts are always bought or sold on this stock and cannot be transferred to other stocks.

Uptrend is an upward price movement of a stock or index. It consists of offsetting higher highs and higher lows.

Volatility is a measurement of price movement. The more point spread in the movement, the greater the volatility. For sector trading, a degree of volatility is needed to create movement.

Working capital ratio is a type of ratio summarizing the health of the company's cash flow and its ability to pay its debts and fund growth from the cash generated by operations.

Bibliography

Stone, Chris. 2005. "Sector Rotation: The Essentials." http://www.in
vestopedia.com/articles/trading/05/020305.asp.

Stovall, Sam. 1996. *Sector Investing: How to Buy the Right Stock in the Right Industry at the Right Time*. New York, New York: McGraw Hill.

The Wagner Daily: www.morpheustrading.com/services.htm

Trading Resource Guide

RECOMMENDED READING

ETF TRADING TACTICS: USING THE POWER OF THE MARKET TO MAKE MONEY – DVD
by David Vomund

Are you missing out on trading the fastest-growing, new investment vehicle?

Join the thousands of investors who already have nearly a half-trillion dollars in Exchange-Traded Funds (ETFs) and get in on the profits of this popular, new financial product that boasts high-liquidity, low fees and lots of diversification. David Vomund's 90-minute presentation gives you everything you need to get started in trading ETFs:

- The basics of ETFs: how they work, their benefits, what makes them so appealing, and why they will eventually over-take mutual funds,

- Techniques for leveraging your ETF investments for profiting in both the short-term and long-term,

- Highly-effective mechanical ETF relative-strength rotation techniques -- style, sector, and international -- that are now available to the individual investor,

- An aggressive strategy for trading sector and international ETFs.

Vomund's rock-solid and simple strategies for evaluating and rotating ETFs will have you on your way to profiting in no time.

Don't get left behind… make ETFs a part of your trading strategy and start seeing returns.

Item #BCDWx5197588- $99.00

ETF TRADING STRATEGIES REVEALED
by David Vomund

Pulling from experts in the field like Linda Bradford Raschke and Steve Palmquist, this book has all the information you need to begin trading ETFs for profit:

- Learn the basics of ETFs; how they work, why they're growing in popularity, and how you can get your share of the profits.

- Discover the way to apply classic techniques to leverage your ETF investments for both the short-term and long-term.

- Study simple but highly effective mechanical ETF rotation techniques (style, sector, and international) that are now available to the individual investor.

ETF Trading Strategies Revealed doesn't end there. Learn from long-time trader and founder of AIQ Systems, Dr. J.D. Smith, what it takes to mentally be the best. When you have the emotional discipline to follow his techniques, you'll find increased profits aren't far behind.

Item #BCDWx4941140 - $19.95

To get the current lowest price on any item listed
Go to www.traderslibrary.com

MASTERING HIGH PROBABILITY CHART READING METHODS WITH JOHN MURPHY – DVD

by John J. Murphy

Post big gains - even if the market is locked in a downward spiral—by following the powerful sector trading strategies of renowned technical analyst John Murphy. The Traders Hall of Fame honoree shows you step-by-step how to pinpoint the right sectors to play at the right time—and how to shift seamlessly from one to the other—with profits in tow. Citing key relationships among markets—from stocks to commodities, bonds to currencies—Murphy's methods help you determine when to move from one to the other so you're poised to capture the most lucrative opportunities available in any market climate. With a full online support manual, Murphy's on-target cues for rotating among sectors will keep you in the "hot" winning ones, at the best points in the business cycle—time after time. *Formally titled: "Simple Sector Trading Strategies: Profit by being in the right markets—at the right time"

Item #BCDWx3309702 - $99.00

PREDICTING MARKET TRENDS – DVD
by Alan Farley

Most traders don't realize how time, more than any other factor, has the most impact on how they make their money.

To master the complexity of our modern financial markets, traders need innovative timing techniques and sound trade management in order to profit. In this 90-minute presentation, the Master Swing Trader, Alan Farley, shows you how to incorporate market trends and timing into every single trade you make.

You'll learn about:

- Marketing timing: intra-day market behaviors and trends—what's behind the price moves,

- Optimizing holding periods through recognizing specific chart patterns,

- Target management: position choices and knowing when to take profits,

- Seasonality: days of the week, options expiration, window dressing and other time-sensitive phenomena that impact the flow of the market.

Farley's strategies for profiting on market trends will help you build the skills you need to succeed as an active trader—incorporate these timing techniques and start making smarter trades today!

Item #BCDWx5197575 - $99.00

EXCHANGE TRADED FUNDS AND E-MINI STOCK INDEX FUTURES
by David Lerman

Introducing a remarkable, versatile new tool that's sweeping the trading world. ETF/E-mini trading volume has soared to record levels, as investors discover that it's ideal for speculating and hedging as well as long-term investing in the broader markets. These index products work together to diversify and balance portfolios—and now the Merc's foremost expert reveals every technique and strategy for trading them successfully. Whether you're short-term or long-term player, a risk taker or conservative investor—there's a strategy for you. Lerman's traveled the globe training investors of all levels to integrate ETF & E-minis into their trading mix. Be one of the first to get his breakthrough book—now at the lowest price anywhere.

Item #BCDWx12503 - $49.95

▲ ▲ ▲ ▲ ▲ ▲

Free 2 Week Trial Offer for U.S. Residents From Investor's Business Daily:

INVESTOR'S BUSINESS DAILY will provide you with the facts, figures, and objective news analysis you need to succeed.

Investor's Business Daily is formatted for a quick and concise read to help you make informed and profitable decisions.

This book, along with other books, is available at discounts that make it realistic to provide it as a gift to your customers, clients, and staff. For more information on these long lasting, cost effective premiums, please call us at (800) 272-2855 or you may email us at sales@traderslibrary.com.